WOMEN AT WORK

WOMEN AT WORK
A Psychologist's Secrets to Getting Ahead in Business

By Dr. Sylvia Senter
with Marguerite Howe, Ph.D.,
and Dr. Don Saco

Coward, McCann & Geoghegan
New York

Library of Congress Cataloging in Publication Data

Senter, Sylvia.
    Women at work.

    Bibliography: p.
    Includes index.
    1. Women in business. 2. Organizational behavior.
I. Howe, Marguerite Beede. II. Title.
HF5500.2.S47   658.4'09'088042   81-19514
ISBN 0-698-11157-5   AACR2

PRINTED IN THE UNITED STATES OF AMERICA

CONTENTS

ACKNOWLEDGMENTS

I want first to express my deepest appreciation to a multitalented behavior therapist and clinician, Dr. Donald A. Saco, of the Department of Psychiatry at New York University Medical School. Friend, colleague, and collaborator on many past projects, his assistance and perseverance with this one were indispensable. His extensive contributions to the theoretical, technical, and clinician portions of the book were invaluable, as were the many patient hours he spent editing the final manuscript.

My appreciation also goes to Marguerite Howe for her creative efforts in this memorable joint venture. She was a valued companion on our long journey, helping to cut through occasional overgrowths of verbiage and keeping us on a clear path of printable prose.

I am indebted to Dr. Joseph Wolpe, Professor of Psychiatry at Temple University School of Medicine, for the superlative training I received under his internship program at the Behavior Therapy Unit at the Eastern Pennsylvania Psychiatric

7

Institute and for the subsequent opportunity to conduct research there. During the internship year and at his June Institutes, Dr. Wolpe assembled some of the world's most prominent behavior therapists to hold seminars. These were unique learning experiences. Although most of the techniques elucidated here are derived from that training and based in part on those "experimentally established paradigms of learning" espoused by Dr. Wolpe, I hasten to inform the reader (and my mentor) that I have taken liberties in adapting them to the specific problems of the women for whom this book is intended.

I am grateful to my husband, Jonas, whose vast experience and knowledge of the world of business I was able to share. Living with a corporate executive and being personally involved in many of his enterprises allowed me privileged views of behind-the-scenes corporation activities. I am equally grateful for his patience, encouragement, and enth support of my own independent enterprise.

My gratitude also goes to the many executive women men whom we interviewed, and to my friends in business for helping me to understand better the problems that exist within the corporate world.

And, of course, I want to thank the women in my workshops as well as those in my private practice for making me realize the need for and encouraging me to write this book.

My thanks to Pat Crowley for her secretarial aid, her typing, her good humor, and her friendship.

And finally I want to acknowledge the support of my agent, Jane Rotrosen, who believed in the timeliness and importance of the book's subject matter. My thanks to her assistant, Don Cleary, for his guidance, and to editor Bill Thompson, for his helpful suggestions and efforts with the preparation and organization of the manuscript in its final stages.

—Sylvia Senter
1982

INTRODUCTION

Now, more than ever, there are greater opportunities for women in business. Government mandate has opened up many executive and management positions, and employers are anxious to fill these places with qualified women. For many of the women who take these jobs, the going is not easy. They have to learn the unspoken rules of business for themselves, usually by observing men. They encounter discrimination because they are women. But discrimination is not their only problem. They are also faced with fears, insecurities, and misconceptions that are the result of being brought up as a woman in our society.

Most women have been raised to be nurturing, sweet, sexy, subservient, supportive and self-effacing. This type of conditioning will not help you succeed as a business executive. It's desirable if you want to be a mother and housewife, but traditional "feminine" responses almost never work when you want to function with men as part of a business team. They lead to misunderstandings and ineffectiveness.

Perhaps you may be responding with typical women's conditioning to the people you work with: Are you overly timid? Do you flirt to get what you want? Or do you act helpless and cute? Maybe you feel uncomfortable giving orders, especially to a man. You may have trouble asking for a good salary. Are you thrown when you feel people don't like you? Do you feel like crying when you get angry or are criticized? There are a host of related problems that arise because women are raised to be "ladies" and "nice little girls."

The business world is essentially a man's club. Its rules—written and unwritten—are largely derived from team sports like football, and its structure resembles the discipline and chain of command of the military. Boys, from the time they are small, are involved in team sports. Very few girls have any comparable experience. Boys are often encouraged to be aggressive and independent. Girls rarely are. In this and dozens of other ways, the average man's childhood conditioning has given him the skills to succeed in business life. A woman's childhood conditioning almost never has.

What can she do about it? More than you might imagine. Usually a woman who goes into business is at a disadvantage, compared to a man, either because she has not yet developed certain skills (ability to motivate other people or to stand up and fight for something she wants, for example) or because she has learned to respond to and handle situations in a manner that is neither appropriate nor effective in business. It may be fine in nonbusiness situations, but can lead to confusion, inefficiency and frustration in the office.

Just as men have learned the behavior that enables them to function successfully in the corporate world, so, too, can women. You can reprogram yourself. Several excellent books have been written explaining the problems women encounter when they enter the corporate playing field. Identifying the problems and knowing how to resolve them, however, are two different things. You may be told that it's important to be part of a team. But how do you overcome the conditioning that keeps you from being able to be part of a team?

That's just one of the questions you'll find answers to in the pages ahead. This book focuses on the specific problems that most women encounter in business because of their "traditional" childhood conditioning. Some of these are:

- Inability to give orders
- Fear of taking risks
- Passivity. Waiting for someone to do it for you
- Inability to cope with rejection
- Panic in the face of authority
- Fear of competition
- Confusion about your sexuality and its place in the office
- Not knowing how to use criticism to your advantage
- Needing to nurture and to be indispensable
- Failing to understand the subtleties of teamwork

On page 49 you will find a questionnaire designed to show you where your trouble spots may lie. Once you've identified them, you can go on to learn the techniques that follow, and apply them to your particular problem.

A number of simple exercises can make it possible for you to replace old responses with new ones that are more effective in business situations. Just as men have been conditioned to behave in certain ways, so you can recondition yourself to respond in a similar manner.

In my practice as a behavior therapist, I worked with many bright and capable women who were experiencing difficulty on the job. Sometimes they were functioning far below their capacity. Often they were unable to rise above a limited, stereotyped work role, such as secretary. Or if they held executive or managerial positions, they felt they were not working at their highest level.

Earlier I had been a student of Dr. Joseph Wolpe of Temple University in Philadelphia, who pioneered the development of behavior therapy in this country. I applied some of the techniques of behavior therapy to these women's problems, with excellent results. In a short time the women reported they were less anxious at work; they were able to perceive situations and people more realistically; they related better to their co-workers and managers in business, and they felt more assertive and effective. I eventually developed a therapy program using behavioral procedures especially suited to businesswomen. These procedures are based on the principle that most of our behavior is learned, and can therefore be unlearned. They are described in this book so that you can study them and apply them to your own problems. They can help you, as they have others, to function more comfortably and effectively in office situations.

A young woman named Anne, for example, who came to me as a client, was working as an executive secretary in a large company. She was sweet and always ready to help anyone in need, and catered to her boss. But she was very dissatisfied with herself. She had been in the same position for eight years. She was afraid to ask for a promotion because she couldn't see herself in a more responsible role. She was fearful of assuming responsibilities and taking risks. She also feared authority figures—her boss, in particular. Anne saw herself as friendly but weak. After practicing several of the behavioral techniques included in this book, she was able to overcome her fears and feel more confident. Eventually she saw herself in a different role. A few months later, when she learned that an opening was coming up, she spoke to her boss and asked for a promotion. She's now working as a manager, with a much larger salary.

Anne used techniques like gradual painless exposure, thought stopping, behavior rehearsal, positive self-statements, and others discussed in this book, which enabled her to shape her own behavior. You'll find that when you change the way you act, others will begin to act differently toward you. Eventually you will be able to develop your own effective managerial style.

But before you go any further, you should examine your priorities. At the present time many women, particularly those who are entering the business world, are receiving double messages. They are in conflict over whether they should be "womanly" women, according to the traditional dictates of our culture, or whether they should be able to take care of themselves. It's a decision each woman has to make.

Ask yourself: What are my priorities? What do I really want out of my life? Before you make any plans for your career, or before you continue with the plans you may already have made, it is a good idea to take a fantasy trip into your own future. This will give you a better idea of just how much you have invested in becoming an autonomous executive or managerial woman.

A woman named Jean, who also came to see me as a client, was very enthusiastic about women's lib, and had made the decision for independence and autonomy. But, as it turned out, she was not really in touch with the fact that although she wanted these things, she also wanted the security of a home and children. When I asked her to imagine herself ten years in the future, she saw herself married to a doctor and living in a suburban home. She added that she had finished five or so years in business and had "proven" herself, but her image of herself as a homemaker showed her real priority was to be loved and cared for, to have security, and to enjoy her family.

I'd like to ask you now to do what Jean did. Take a moment to relax, lie back, close your eyes. If you can, be in a place where you won't be disturbed. Imagine yourself ten years from now. See yourself as you go about your usual day. What are your activities? What is your schedule like? Create these images in detail. What's the source of your income? What's your economic bracket? What people are close to you? When you take time off, what do you do for fun? Now you're going out with your friends. What are they like? What kind of clothes do you prefer to wear? What kind of person or persons do you live with? Do you have children? If you do, does your partner share the household duties or the child-raising chores with you? Who's supporting the household? If you are a working woman, does the man you live with respect your work? Do you spend a lot of time at your job? How much of your energy is devoted to business? If you are going to be in a management or executive position, the person you live with will have to realize that your work must often come first. He must be willing to sacrifice or help out at home when necessary. This is an important fact to consider, because some men may not be happy with this kind of arrangement. Many successful businesswomen decide not to have children because their jobs demand a great deal of their energy and attention. How do you feel about this?

If you have answered all these questions thoughtfully and feel that the challenge of a management or executive position is what you want, this book will help you.

I want to emphasize that while the techniques in this book are highly effective, they're not cure-alls. They can't change the fact that you may have a boss who's a male chauvinist, or alter the reality that many important deals are still closed in the steam room. But they can change your reactions, so that certain things don't throw you off your stride. They'll enable you to keep your self-confidence when the customer looks for the boss and is disappointed to find out it's you; when you go to a meeting and the president swears and then turns to you and apologizes, calling attention to the fact that you don't belong in the male club; or when a client refuses to believe you because you're a woman; or when you discover that information is deliberately being passed around you.

If you invest a little time in these techniques they will work for you. They'll help you become more confident, effective, and organized. They'll help you if you're afraid to ask for a raise; if you find you're doing other people's work for them; if you feel trapped in a job that's not challenging; if you feel like crying whenever you're criticized; if men at work keep coming on to you.

You don't need to be a victim. You can learn to handle these and other situations effectively. The first step is to become aware of your own conditioning: It isn't entirely your fault if you've got a problem.

WOMEN'S AND MEN'S CONDITIONING AS CHILDREN

1

Lynn came into her company's marketing department as an assistant product manager. She worked very hard at her job, staying late and on weekends, and was extremely competent. She wanted to be promoted to product manager. But when the promotion she wanted came up, it was given to a man who was not nearly as competent, who had been with the firm less time, but was an old college buddy of the boss.

She became very discouraged and lost her confidence. Her first reaction was that it "wasn't fair." Eventually her work suffered, because she thought no matter how hard she tried it didn't matter—the system was against her. A few months later she left the company and went looking for another job.

The men she worked with were surprised when she quit. They thought Lynn was acting rashly and being too emotional. Many of them had been passed over for promotions at one time or another. They were unhappy when they weren't promoted, but they weren't as devastated as she was. They thought she was sabotaging her own career by leaving.

Why did Lynn and the men she worked with see the same situation differently? Many women fail in business for the same reason Lynn did. They don't understand how the game is played, or its rules. They fail to see that corporate business, being male dominated, has rules created by men to suit their needs, and that men understand the system because they were conditioned to function within these rules from the time they were small boys.

Women, having had very different conditioning, frequently respond in ways that are puzzling to men. In a sense, men and women are raised in two different subcultures. They expect different things, value different things, appraise situations differently. Even many words don't mean the same thing to men and women. But often they don't know it; somehow they assume the other sex sees things the way they do, and are confused when this turns out not to be true.

The men Lynn worked with were puzzled and looked down on her for quitting because she made several mistakes they had learned to avoid when they were boys. She let one defeat get her down. She took it personally. She hadn't expected it. She'd also concentrated on getting her job done perfectly rather than making friends with the right people.

Lynn felt the company should have recognized her merits, and when it didn't, she felt that "justice" wasn't being done. The men, on the other hand, thought that this was all perfectly within the rules. She also felt her performance on the job was not the company's criterion for promotion, and that confused her. She had done a "perfect" job in her section, focusing on details, being an expert. The boss's school chum seemed to her like a goof-off. He did his job sloppily and nosed around in other departments, went out to lunch a lot, and played tennis with the boys. It was true he was pretty gung-ho about the company, whereas she would occasionally gripe about company policy, but she figured that because she did her job so well she had a right to complain once in a while when things were done inefficiently. She began to attribute her being passed over to discrimination because she was a woman. Finally she got so angry and depressed she began to hate the job and everyone connected with it.

The roots of Lynn's problems can be traced back to her childhood. She was responding as many women would in her situation, because conditioning has not prepared them to be managers or executives in the corporate world. Lynn ran into trouble because women and men, from the beginning of their lives, are taught to relate to their environment in different ways, as society prepares them for different roles in life.

The first question usually asked about a baby is, Is it a boy or a girl? Your gender stays with you, the most essential part of your identity, for the rest of your life. You were conditioned to behave in a way appropriate to your sex from the moment you were born.

We are all conditioned by other people, especially by our parents, who shape our behavior—actively encouraging, discouraging, or ignoring it. We imitate them as role models. We are also conditioned by peer pressure, which usually becomes important at about age five or six.

Stop and think about yourself for a minute. Why do you walk and sit the way you do, instead of like a truck driver, with legs apart and hands on your knees? Why don't you slap other women on the shoulder when you greet them? Why do you tend to speak softly? Maybe feel the impulse to clear the table and wash the dishes? Sometimes cry at a movie? Try to smooth things over if people squabble? Coo and talk baby talk to a baby? Panic when you see a snake? Wish you were younger or thinner or prettier? Get upset when a cabbie is rude to you? Talk about clothes instead of football when you get together with a friend?

Our physical responses and mannerisms as well as our emotional makeup are influenced by the way we have been treated since childhood. As little girls we get different messages from the ones boys get: "You're my little girl! Tell me if anyone hurts you and I'll take care of him!" But if somebody picks on a boy, his father is likely to say, "Go out and fight your own battles. Go beat 'em up! You have to learn to take care of yourself." This attitude encourages the boy to have a sense of self-reliance. He feels he can have an effect on his environment. If something of a girl's gets broken, she runs to daddy to mend it. If a boy's toy gets broken, his father will probably teach him how to fix it. A girl is encouraged to depend on others to take care of her. She's looking for a rescuer—a knight on a white charger. The boy gets the message: *You can do it.* But the girl gets the message: *I'll do it for you. You're helpless.* Often if a girl does become competent, learns to use tools, build a tree house, wrestle, or box, she's accused of being a tomboy, which has a negative connotation.

"Why don't you help your sister with that?" the boy may hear. "Aren't you a gentleman?" So he watches over his sister. He learns to be protective. She hits him and he hits her back, and he's told, "She's just a little girl. You don't do that to little girls." The little girl gets the message that she's easily hurt, fragile. That it's a terrible thing to hurt herself. Many mothers will say, "I watch out for her all the time," or "I worry about her going out alone." But, "He's been out on his own since he was eight," they say proudly. "He's very self-sufficient. He's always been able to take care of himself."

Parents may tell a daughter, "Don't talk to strangers." And she becomes more timid and less sure about the world out there. A little boy may get the underlying message he's in charge of the household if anything happens to his father. He will take care of his mother and sister. This is rarely true of a daughter.

One father explained how he reacted differently to his son and daughter when they were in similar situations. His daughter, who was about ten, was being pushed around by a bullying girl in her class. She complained to her father many times and he told her to ignore it. Finally the little girl said, "She's started to push me hard." The father told her, "The next time she does it just push her back." Later he said to me, "I was worried sick about it, because they might fight and she might get a cut on her face, and her looks would be ruined. But when it was my son in a situation like that, I told him to give the kid one hard, fast punch in the nose. But I didn't worry about it. I thought, If he gets a scar on his face it's okay. It looks masculine."

Boys, from a very early age, get the message: *You'll have to support yourself when you grow up, so go out and learn how to take care of yourself.* The message the girl gets is very different. One study* showed that in many of the books used to teach reading in grade schools, when something good happened to a male character in the story it was always the result of his own actions. When something good happened to a female character, of which there were far fewer, it was because someone did it for her, gave her something, or because she was lucky.

You can't take care of yourself. Find someone to support you is the message little girls get. Girls learn very early that it's important to look nice and be pleasing, that little girls should be dainty and sweet, have good manners, be graceful, be princesses.

As a child you got clothes for your dolls. Your toys emphasized appearance: You played dress-up in mommy's high heels. You put on lipstick. Boys rarely get toys that make them conscious of appearance. Their toys are much more active. They get baseball mitts, bats, guns, trains, bricks, trucks, airplanes, building kits.

A girl's looks are important because she is told she's got to find the best possible husband to support her. Her stock in trade is being beautiful and pleasing, knowing how to handle

*C. N. Jacklin and H. N. Mischel, "As the Twig Is Bent: Sex Role Stereotyping in Early Readers," *School Psychology Digest* 2 (1973) 30–37.

men, making them comfortable, taking care of them, making them want her. A girl grows up with the sense that she is waiting to be chosen. She is Cinderella waiting for the prince with the glass slipper. This kind of mentality contributes to a lack of initiative when she's a grown woman. She doesn't get the message that she can go out there and fend for herself, that she can go out there and fight.

We judge our value as women by how much we are liked, rather than by how competent we are. Men judge their worth by how much respect they get for their accomplishments. But women are afraid not to have people like them. They depend on approval for their sense of self-worth.

Often it is important to a father that his son be a good athlete. He's got to be a ballplayer or he'll be a "sissy." "I'm embarrassed," said one father, "when my son isn't a good ballplayer. I go to some of the games out of a sense of duty. But I'd go to all of them if he were better." And when the son scores a run, he hears, "I'm proud of you."

The same father reinforces different things in his daughter. He buys her pretty clothes. He cuddles her for being sweet. He watches her brush her hair with admiration. He likes her feminine walk. He enjoys the fact that she always looks immaculate, like a "dream." "That's my daughter. She always looks *perfect*. Always smells so nice." And when she goes out on dates, her dress is very important. She's dainty and delicate. "I want my daughter to be a lady," he said.

In fairy tales the heroine is always a beautiful princess who gets the prince who rides up in shining armor to kill the dragon and *rescue* this fragile, lovely creature. The women in fairy tales who aren't beautiful are witches, stepmothers, and stepsisters. This leads children to conclude that if you are beautiful you are good, loveable, and desirable. If you are ugly, you are evil, a loser, unwanted, and unloved.

Sometimes this conditioning leads to the Jewish Princess syndrome, where a girl expects the world to be at her feet just because she's physically attractive. The other side of this is her sense that no matter how nice she looks she never looks beautiful enough. Someone else is always better.

Boys learn from their games that their value to the team depends on their actions and skills. When they grow up they can be richer, win more prizes, and play better than others. But their value depends on what they are *doing*. Girls, because they're judged for their attractiveness, tend to feel their value depends on what they *are*, rather than what they do. They become caught up in perfecting themselves. They're never thin enough, they're never pretty enough, they're never stylish enough. They spend a lot of time on their appearance trying to make themselves "perfect."

Their games are often variations of the ballet class, which are aimed at perfecting the body as pleasing and an end in itself. Grown women usually play sports for "exercise." They don't play to win. A boy may practice to perfect a skill but he will probably do so to use it in competition.

One of the ways women and men are differently conditioned is through the games they play as children. Boys tend to play on clubs and teams. Girls play one to one. Growing up you probably had a best friend—a girl who was like a sister, more important than anyone else. You usually had an exclusive relationship. You couldn't have two "best" friends at the same time. Most girls tend to pick best friends who are like themselves: stylish if they're stylish, popular if they're popular, bookish if they're bookish. A little girl's best friend can't be too much better than she is, either. She doesn't want the competition. That's too hard on her ego. On the other hand, people judge you by your friends, so she has to be careful. Sometimes a less popular friend can bring her down in status.

The relationship is a secure place; it's you and your friend against the world. Other girls are excluded. This encourages intolerance. You and your friend get picky. You get the habit of criticizing others, harping on their faults. Girls like to gossip about each other. They can be "catty."

Boys usually have a very different experience. They tend to form clubs and teams. They run in gangs spontaneously. From Little League, football, social clubs, and the packs that little boys love with their own rules, they develop a sense of teamwork and cooperation over the years. They go on camping trips together. They're encouraged to stay in groups and often discouraged from the one-to-one relationships acceptable for girls. Parents get concerned if a boy continually sleeps over at another boy's house, but it's encouraged among girls.

Boys learn very early that you need a certain number of players to make a team, and if you want to be on the team you'd better get along with them all, whether you like them or not. They learn to overlook the flaws in their teammates. They come to believe that nobody's perfect. But the little girl is encouraged to be selective and exclusive: "I only associate with people I like."

Usually a woman's good friend is around her own age and has similar interests. Not always so for a man. A "guy" is anyone over twenty-one with whom he may play ball or cards. The important thing is the camaraderie, the sense of being one of a bunch. Friendships for women tend to be an end in themselves. When a woman goes shopping she'll take along a friend she feels comfortable with. It's one to one. This is why some women are puzzled when a man will continue to be friends with someone he doesn't approve of or even get along with. "Then why do you play ball with him?" she asks. "Because he's my buddy, and nobody's perfect."

Organizations like the Girl Scouts are not as important to girls as boys' organizations and clubs are to them. For boys these experiences provide training in mutual effort and cooperation. A boy learns, probably when he's about six, that since it's a world that forms groups, he'd better join the best group, and learn to get along with it. But a little girl learns that she's going to be a loner. It's her against the rest of the women, competing for the prize: the best man. All other women are her potential rivals.

In boys' groups the pecking order is usually based on intelligence, athletic skill, ability to get along with others, and, when they're older, on popularity with girls. A girl's place in the pecking order depends on how popular she is, how pretty, how stylish, and how socially adept she is.

Most women think of competition as something negative. To be "competitive" isn't nice. Essentially, competition is against other women for acceptance, for "the prize" of a husband. It's a big popularity contest. The women girls see as winning—Miss America or movie stars—are chosen because of their beauty and their agreeableness. And these role models—our heroines—are loners. Competition is something that alienates you from other women. You get the message you're a lone star up there in your own firmament. It's you against the world, there's no sense of team cooperation.

The little boy learns that competition is usually part of a team effort. It's a chance to prove himself, a welcome challenge. His heroes are O. J. Simpson and Joe Namath, both members of teams. When he grows up he wants to be a policeman or a fireman, also part of a team. Men are turned on by competition. It stimulates them. They like a crisis or a challenge because they feel that otherwise there's no test of their skills, and they get bored.

A boy develops the sense that fundamentally, where competition is involved, it's all a game. His acts, his skills, his performance are on the line, and need proving. But not himself. If he loses, he figures he'll get another chance to prove himself in the next game. A little girl develops the sense that if she loses, her personal value is lowered. She's a failure. She's of no value. She won't get a second chance. She's annihilated. She's developed no sense that it's a game.

She hasn't learned the important lesson that boys learn: *You win some, you lose some.* A boy doesn't become discouraged easily if he loses. He usually analyzes what he did wrong, tries to improve his performance, and strives to win the next time. But women fear failure because they think that they won't have another chance. They haven't learned that *you can't win 'em all.*

Because the boy is used to having his performance evaluated on teams, he learns not to be devastated by criticism. Everyone on a team is criticized after a game to improve their performance. He learns to use it to his own benefit. The girl views criticism as a put-down. When she grows up, she takes it as rejection.

A boy knows from his team sports that every game is a calculated gamble. He appraises the field, his own strengths and weaknesses, the strengths and weaknesses of the other players, and he does his best. If there's a chance to prove himself, he's willing to take the risk. He learns that taking risks often pays off: You may win the game. He's also encouraged to take risks in other areas. If he climbs a tree and falls out of it and hurts himself, he hears, "Good for you, at least you tried." But if a little girl attempts to climb a tree, she's likely to be told, "Be careful, you'll hurt yourself." She gets the message: *You need taking care of. You're fragile.* She becomes overcautious. She wants to play it safe. When she grows up she'll probably associate risk with losing something or being hurt, unlike her brother, who'll see it as a chance to gain something. Every down in a football game is a calculated gamble. And he knows if he loses this one he'll try again on the next one.

A girl's conditioning encourages her to be perfect in limited endeavors. When she's little and does a small task well she's rewarded, so she's careful about details from then on. She's told it's nice to neaten things up, and tie up loose ends. She's probably criticized if her room is a mess. She's taught to play house with dolls, to sew, to cook—all precise little activities. When she grows up, she'll tend to do little jobs perfectly.

Her games are aimed at self-perfection. Jump rope, hopscotch, jacks. She's really not competing against other girls, she's competing against herself to perfect her skill or to top her previous performance. A boy, because he's on a team, is taught to focus not on the performance but on the goal. He doesn't care about the details so much. He's *goal oriented.* If his room is a mess he's probably not as seriously criticized as his sister.

From their games boys also develop a completely different sense of what rules are and what they're used for. When they're about eight, they learn that rules are impersonal and apply to everybody. They usually like to discuss what's "fair," and argue about the rules. In many sports, like football, a good player knows how far he can bend the rules without breaking them. In football, if you legally deceive an opponent it is considered admirable.

Girls' games emphasize skills, not rules. Often the "rules" are something they agree upon between themselves. Girls tend to identify the rules with the authority figures who enforce them. They don't develop any sense of an impersonal, working system within which they function. A girl believes that it's not as important to win the game as it is to play it "fairly." The closer you stick with the rules, the better you play. She develops a romantic, idealized notion of what things "should" be like, while her brother is out there analyzing the playing field, looking at his opponent's strengths and weaknesses and his own, in an attempt to *win the game.* He learns to be a realist, attuned to his environment. He has to be able to predict what's going to happen. A girl is more likely to be idealistic. She's never needed to use much strategy, because she's basically competing with herself. Her ladylike games will teach her to be more attuned to her body, her inner states, and her solo performance.

Sometimes a little girl wants to get something from a parent, and when she's refused, she cries or has a tantrum. Frequently the parent relents. Or if she falls down and hurts herself, an adult may run and hug her, give her a Band-Aid, hold her in his or her lap. She's encouraged to display her feelings, and learns to use her emotions to get what she wants and to manipulate people. If a boy acts the same way, his father will tell him, "Big boys don't cry." Men, consequently, view emotionality as an inability to control oneself, an inability to behave rationally. If a boy gets upset in a football game, he may cause the team to lose. He's encouraged not to show anger when he's replaced on the field. He is expected to be a "good sport." If a girl's emotional, she's usually protected: "Oh, you know, she's just a girl." "Women are like that." Consequently, a woman's decision making is often quite emotional. She lets her heart rule her head. "If you really *want* to do something . . ." "If it doesn't *feel* right to you . . ." She goes on a gut reaction, when a man would probably say, "Give me the facts." "What's the bottom line?" "This doesn't make sense." He analyzes. He has a different sense from hers of what justifies an action. He may be amazed when she follows her feelings in making a decision.

A girl is not encouraged to act aggressive or angry. She learns to express her anger by crying, sulking, or withdrawing. In general, angry boys are encouraged to hit out, to "stick up for their rights," to be much more physical. If you see two boys fighting, the crowd is probably cheering them on. Often boys relieve their hostility by yelling at each other. A girl is more likely to express her aggression indirectly. A man in an extreme situation will probably get physical and fight if he has to; a woman, almost never. There are few, if any, women prizefighters.

A girl is encouraged to be nurturing. She's trained to be a little hostess. She gets a tea set for Christmas. Her dolls visit each other. She may have a baking kit, a makeup kit, a little stove and a little iron and a little dishwasher. She learns by imitating mommy that she should want to make it all better for everyone. It makes her feel necessary. She'll take care of her doll, she'll take care of the cat. She will get the nurse kit. She's been taught to sacrifice. She's Florence Nightingale. She's mommy's little helper.

Little boys often experiment with cruelty. They may pull insects apart or tie cans on the tail of a dog. When they grow up this cruelty takes the form of a detachedness. They may be more impersonal, objective, or insensitive. Men don't feel sorry as easily. They don't pity or empathize as women have been taught to do. Boys play at war in the vacant lot. They "kill" each other with guns. They are not Florence Nightingale, but General MacArthur.

Girls are generally shunted into the role of spectator and appreciator. The boy's activities are already seen as more important than hers. This may be because it is understood that a boy is going to have to go out and support himself and a family, while a girl's ability to support herself is optional. Should she have a goal it is often to be a teacher, nurse, or secretary until she gets married.

If you think back on your own grade school you may remember how the girls were usually the audience for the boys. They laughed at and applauded the boys, who were given the center stage either as heroes or clowns. The girls were not encouraged to take an active role. The best example of this is cheerleaders. A cheerleader is cute and pretty. She cheers the boys on. You never see the boys cheering for the girls. The girls applaud the heroes on the football field, no matter how rough, how dirty, how brutal. They are the ones to be admired.

In the lower grades girls are usually more academically adept than boys. But girls start to perform less well at adolescence, because they don't want to compete with boys. Academic excellence for a girl often means that she is "teacher's pet." A "pet" is no threat to the boys' masculinity.

A popular girl, when you were growing up, was probably smart or pretty, or both. When a boy was too smart in school he was usually picked on by the other boys. To be popular, a boy had to be athletic, or one of the gang—easy to get along with. A "good guy." The girls could be little snobs, but if they were pretty and smart, they were popular. The boys were the ones who used to get into trouble. They weren't discouraged from being "roughnecks"; they were reinforced because it got them attention. There was always a class Romeo, a class dunce, and a class clown. You probably can't think of the class clown as a girl. Girls appreciated; they were passive spectators.

Although a lot of young people today aren't raised according to the old double standard, the traditional roles when many of us were growing up were stricter. If a girl slept around she was "loose." We all knew there were nice girls and bad girls. Implicitly, a girl had to keep herself "pure" so she'd have more market value: Men didn't usually marry loose women. But if her brother "scored" he was a "make-out artist." He got peer approval for it. His sister had to be home by twelve if she was out on a date, but he could come in when he wanted. "If she was shacked up I'd be ticked off," said one father. "But if my son did it, no big deal." These are the old standards, but a lot of them still prevail in more subtle forms.

Girls and boys also develop different attitudes towards money. The average girl probably gets an allowance. Maybe she gets her allowance for being "good," for helping her mother, for doing the dishes, or taking over the roles her mother has. She rarely has a job outside of her home. If she is to work as a baby-sitter, it's not until she's a teenager; earlier in life she's financially dependent on her parents. Even when she earns money it's usually in a domestic capacity. The basis for this may be the fear that the girl might be molested if she's away from home at a job.

A boy, on the other hand, has an allowance that's usually contingent on jobs that he does at home and outside the home.

He learns very early that his work can be exchanged for money. It seems like a natural thing, because his father, who's his role model, is the money earner in the family, and he expects some day to be a breadwinner too. He's stimulated more by ideas about how he can earn money: delivering papers, cutting grass, working after school, or shoveling snow. He learns his services are worth money, and develops a sense of financial independence. If he cuts the neighbor's lawn, he gets two dollars. If he doesn't cut the lawn, he doesn't get the two dollars. He takes his job-earning ability seriously. But the little girl's allowance is a general sustenance for being "good." She often doesn't see the connection between her efforts and their monetary value.

There are some women who, because of their conditioning as children, can function in the business world more easily than others. In the majority of cases these women had very supportive fathers who gave them the message as little girls that they could do anything they set out to do.* Sometimes a girl was a substitute son for the father. He took her out to ball games, brought her along when he visited his buddies, and often made her his companion. When these little girls grew up, they became independent, proud of their skill in sports, enjoyed playing on teams, and often were unhappy when they were restricted to "girls' games" in school. They were encouraged to think things through for themselves and to take risks.

But most of us did not have this type of relationship or conditioning; we aren't as secure, confident, or comfortable in the rough-and-tumble corporate world.

*Margaret Hennig and Anne Jardim, *The Managerial Woman.* Doubleday, 1976.

CONDITIONING: HELP OR HINDRANCE IN CORPORATE LIFE

2

As we have seen, traditional conditioning prepares men for the corporate structure while it works against women in the same situation. As a working woman you may be having problems at work for this reason. Increase your awareness of the subtle difference in the way men and women behave. Watch people in operation. Some of the problems that follow apply to both sexes, but are more common among women raised with the conditioning we discussed in the previous chapter.

PERFECTIONISM

If you have this tendency, you focus only on the job you're doing, and you do it perfectly. You worry about details. You can't delegate responsibility because you don't trust other people to do the job. Protecting and perfecting what you have, you don't look at how each task relates to your overall strategy, what's "in it" for you, or where your next move is. You

31

want to be indispensable. You become identified with the job. If you're such a good secretary, nobody wants you to be anything else. You're myopic about your career.

Sally was a straight-A student in college and did very well in business school, so she was snapped up by a prestigious fast-food corporation eager for competent women. Her entry position was assistant to the comptroller. Sally did her homework and became very efficient. She was an excellent assistant—so much so that she was overloaded with work. But there was no increase in her title and no raise for the extra responsibilities. She became dissatisfied. If there was an extra task around, her bosses would say: "Why don't you give it to Sally? She'll do a good job." And that was true. Sally would do a nearly perfect job in everything she did, even though it took her twice as much time.

She would be working at her desk overtime while the other women were waiting for the clock to reach five so they could leave. She often worked late. She would look around and feel there was something wrong. She knew they weren't working as hard as she but they still seemed to be valued as much as she was. Other people would finish a job adequately and leave; they would get just as much appreciation. She wasn't getting anything extra for working so hard.

Sally was such a perfectionist that she couldn't delegate authority, so she did everything herself. The message she gave herself was: "Everything that comes through me must be perfect. I'll see that it's perfect." If it wasn't perfect, she felt anxious.

When I met her, she was a trim, impeccably dressed, crisp, auburn-haired young woman, who felt she was overloaded with work. She was harassed, highly anxious, and depressed because she felt the situation was impossible. She felt helpless about it.

She told me that as a girl she was well behaved, easy to get along with, and pleasant. She was always praised by her father for doing little things well: setting the table, dressing her dolls, doing the dishes. That was her identity; she was reinforced for doing each little job perfectly.

As an adult Sally was a little myopic; she saw each job separately, and her identity was involved with each task as it came up.

A man, in contrast, has been trained to see things as a whole from the time he was a child. In a football game, for example, he focuses on a long-term goal: winning the game. He does his best in each play, but his whole identity isn't tied up in it. As a result, when a boy grows up, he does his job adequately but always with an eye on the next step, the distant goal, and what maneuvers he needs to make. Who can he use to get there? What does he need to know?

FAILURE TO CREATE LONG-RANGE CAREER PLANS

You drift. You can't visualize yourself in an executive capacity. You can't make five- or ten-year plans. You have a big investment in the status quo and security. You're so focused on the present you don't have time or energy to focus on the future.

If this is true of you, then possibly, like many women, you were conditioned to think that if your career didn't work out you could always get married. Eventually someone would take care of you, so you didn't have to work or think as hard as you would otherwise. "I don't see myself doing this for the rest of my life. I'll be married or have other things to do."

A man doesn't have that out. From the time he's a boy a man has the incentive of knowing that he must go out and support himself as an adult. He gets the message: No one's going to support you.

LOW EXPECTATIONS OF YOURSELF

You're unable to see yourself as a big success out there. Something holds you back. Someone has created an image in your mind that you're inferior. You feel funny about selling yourself because you think you're lying—you don't believe in yourself. You're willing to settle for less money or less prestige. You think small. You'll do an executive job with administrative pay and a lesser title.

Bonnie was brought up in a family where her parents said there wasn't enough money for her to go to college. They had saved so her brother could go to a university because he had to support himself. He had to *be* something. When she wanted to go to college, her parents said she could go to secretarial school. Before she raised the subject they never even mentioned that she might continue her schooling.

A man's life-style depends on the career he chooses. Skilled jobs bring higher income. As a boy, when he went out to do something, like sell newspapers, he expected to be paid for it. When a girl helped her mother in the kitchen, she was patted on the head and told she was a good girl. She didn't get paid for what she did.

When you've been treated like a second-class citizen you don't develop high aspirations. You grow up with a limited view of where you're going and you accept it.

PASSIVITY

You want to be feminine and beautiful. Your passivity is reinforced by fairy tales and stereotypes: "I have to be pretty." If you are good and attractive, someone will take care of you.

As a result you may go to your job expecting the boss to automatically promote you. A magical person will discover you. You don't make plans for yourself or don't take responsibility for getting ahead.

When something good happens to you—a good job, promotion, award—you feel that someone else did it for you. It happens *to* you. You don't believe that you did it yourself, so you don't take yourself seriously.

In corporate life, *you* make things happen for yourself.

Ruth was assistant to the director of purchases at a well-known furniture manufacturing firm. She was pleasant and got along well with everybody. She kept a very low profile. But when promotions came around she was always overlooked. The years went by and a woman who had come to work for her as her assistant was promoted over her. She later found out that the woman had asked for the promotion. Ruth wondered why others moved past her. She was more competent than they. But she was more passive: waiting for someone to see how good she was and promote her. Ruth did her job, minded her own business, and waited for recognition. She is still waiting.

When she was growing up, Ruth was mama's little girl. Whenever her mother, who was usually passive, would stand up to her father, he would say, "Keep your place. I don't like a pushy woman." So Ruth grew up with the idea that a woman who is aggressive gets criticized and punished.

In contrast, a boy might go to his father and say, "Dad, would you fix this for me?" His dad says, "No, you do it yourself," or "I'll show you how it's done so you can do it yourself later." He learns as a child, "If I want something done, I've got to do it myself." He develops, instead of passivity, a sense of doing and causing things to happen. "I can do it. I'll take care of it." As he sees the evidence of his effectiveness, he will be motivated to take on other challenges. Later in life when he has successes there will be no doubt in his mind that he was responsible for them.

FEAR OF RISK

If you are afraid of taking risks, you won't be willing to leave a safe, comfortable job and go into a situation where you may or may not succeed. You have trouble making decisions. You won't take a promotion even if it's offered to you because you're afraid you won't do well.

Kathy was a bright, attractive blond in her thirties, who went from one meaningless job to another. Because she decided she wanted to specialize, she went back to school and took courses in financing and investing. She thought in terms of money until it became second nature to her. Then she was hired by an investment firm on Wall Street. She stayed for two years, learned all the ins and outs, and was well known on the floor of the stock exchange. An opportunity came up when one of the partners died and she was given a chance to take his seat. She turned it down. She feared that if she failed she would be humiliated and people would look down on her. She'd have to give back the seat and her career would be ruined. It would be known on the stock exchange that she had failed. It was just too much of a risk for her.

Kathy, like most women, had grown up to be cautious and fearful of situations involving risk.

Men look for chances to take risks. As boys, one might hear from another: "I dare you to do it." And if he doesn't do it he's a "sissy." A boy is always trying to top the other kids. He gets attention for doing risky things; little girls giggle and make a fuss over him. Boys call each other "chicken" if they don't take a dare.

A man sees risk as opportunity: a chance for winning or gaining. Boys are taught to play the kind of games where if you don't take a risk, you won't have the chance to get what you want. A boy climbs a tree and gets approval: "He's all boy." Boys dare each other to take risks constantly, but challenge usually isn't part of a girl's vocabulary. Girls are encouraged to play house and other safe games. Basically a girl sees risk as a threat: a chance to be hurt or to lose something. Every time she tries to do something risky, she's told to "Be careful."

BEING SHATTERED BY LOSING

You're discouraged because you failed to get a promotion or because you lost an account. As a result you stop trying. You give up. No one likes to lose, but women are usually more devastated by failure than men.

If a little girl loses, she sulks and goes home and gets sympathy for it. She is rewarded by consolation. Whenever someone hurts her, she's reassured and protected. She's sheltered, so she's afraid to take chances. In effect, she's rewarded for losing by getting positive attention.

When little boys lose they are spurred on to go out and try again until they win. "Get out there and fight." If Johnny gets beaten up, he is told: "Go out and beat *him* up." Because "the game" is an important part of the boy's life, it's accepted that he will win some and lose some. He may get upset, but he knows there's always a next time, and another chance to be a winner.

REJECTION

You get upset if everybody doesn't like you. If a colleague ignores you, you feel put down. To you it means there's something wrong with you. You quit a great job just because your boss isn't easy to get along with. He doesn't give you approval or positive feedback. You're afraid to ask for promotions because you're afraid your peers may not like it. You need constant approval and assurance that you're worthwhile. The message you're giving is, Please like me.

Girls are taught to be sweet, likable, and polite. They are dependent on the approval of others. It's important for them to be popular.

A boy, on the other hand, doesn't care if someone doesn't like him. He may even encourage some people to fear him. The most important thing for him is to get respect. If a boy loses his temper, he's being a boy. If a girl does the same thing, she's not being a "lady." A man, then, is not destroyed by rejection. He may be put out of action temporarily, but he's quick to recover. He may even view it as a learning experience or a signal to try harder. A man wants respect; a woman wants to be liked.

COMPETITION

You won't make an effort to compete for a certain job if someone you consider very capable is going after it too. You won't venture into a bigger fish pond, preferring to stay a big fish in a small one. You may not want to leave your small town for a big city where there's more competition, or your present job for a bigger company making a better product.

Men, on the other hand, are usually stimulated by competition. They love a good scramble. Games or business are competitive and exciting chances to prove oneself.

In school, little girls don't usually compete with boys for grades or in sports, because they feel the boys won't like them. A lot of women feel ambivalent about competing with men. They view competition as threatening. How many women feel comfortable taking a higher-paying job than their husbands? Women are often punished by men for winning, so they prefer to fail. A woman may be uncomfortable with competition because she believes it's unfeminine.

CRITICISM

Your boss tells you you handed in an incomplete report, and you're crushed. You feel as if it's you being judged, not your performance. You're so caught up in your reaction you can't analyze what the boss is saying.

Lucille gave a report that the boss cut to shreds in front of her colleagues. What she heard was: "You're no good." What he really was saying was: "This report needs to be changed." She was confused later when he came up to her in a friendly way and, as if nothing had happened, chatted about whether she was happy with the travel arrangements for a business trip she was about to make. She didn't realize that in the meeting he was only attacking the job she had done, not her.

When a girl is criticized, she takes it as a personal rejection. It means she's worthless. Boys learn to accept criticism in team sports, where it's given to help them improve their game. They can separate themselves from their performance. A girl is more sheltered from criticism and rarely learns to accept it as an aid to personal growth.

NURTURING (BEING MOTHER HEN)

You keep helping an incompetent subordinate to do his job. You're the shoulder for others to cry on. You give advice and do serving tasks, like getting coffee and running errands for others.

Everyone in the office came to Helen with their problems. She'd been in business before she had children, and after her children grew up she went back. She was very organized, knew her field well, and was a hard worker. She was proud of the fact that she was well liked in the office. Trouble arose when she found herself frequently working late helping people with their jobs or doing favors for them. A lot of her work time was consumed giving advice. She enjoyed helping people. She felt important at first, but eventually their demands became a burden. She started feeling swamped, and guilty if she said no. After a while she began to resent her co-workers, and felt as if they were taking pieces out of her.

Boys are not taught to be nurturing. It's accepted as normal if they get into fights, go fishing, or play practical jokes at Halloween. They learn to be impersonal, even cruel. They play games like war, and Cowboys and Indians. In corporate life a man's first concern is getting the job done. For many men, the personal needs of others come second, if at all.

EMOTIONALITY

You want to cry in meetings. You lose your temper and scream at people. You constantly lose your cool, or cry when the boss hollers at you.

Terry was sales rep for a thriving computer software company. After she had made a presentation at a regional meeting the sales director said, "I had expected a better job from you. You didn't seem very well prepared." She got extremely upset and quickly left the meeting to go to the ladies' room, where she had a good cry.

Crying is the most effective strategy little girls have. Who can resist a little girl who's about to dissolve into tears? She seems so helpless. Her brothers are likely to hear, "Big boys don't cry." Being called "cool" is a compliment. It means you don't show your emotions. Most men carefully guard their personal feelings and don't allow any place for them in business.

TRADING ON YOUR SEXUALITY

You flirt and use sex to get what you want. You lean on sexuality to gain a point. Whenever you're unsure, you use your feminine wiles. If this sounds like you, perhaps you've learned to be seductive to get what you want.

Betsy dressed in a very appealing manner. She smiled a little more than she needed to; her movements were overly feminine and slightly suggestive. She wasn't too well liked by other women in the office. She was frequently seen speaking to the men, and she felt she had an "in" with them. She couldn't understand why, when they were reorganizing the office, she was let go. The boss had obviously interpreted her behavior as frivolous. She did not project the businesslike image he expected of his employees.

As a little girl, when Betsy wanted to get around her father she would smile sweetly at him and climb onto his lap and stroke his face. She learned that that was the way to get what she wanted. "She's such a little flirt. She'll have a million boyfriends when she grows up," are meant as compliments to the little girl.

A man does not learn to rely on sex to get what he wants. As a boy he is discouraged from being manipulative. He is told to ask for it "like a man," to be straightforward. A girl is often encouraged to be coy, indirect, and flirtatious.

THE SEXUAL PUT-DOWN

You feel sexually put down or used as a sex object when men call you "honey," "sweetheart," "doll," etc. You're upset when you're tested for availability by male colleagues. It's as if they are saying: "Keep your place as a woman."

Maggie was a management trainee for a soft-drink distribution firm. She became upset and irritated when men called her "sweetie" or "hon" at the office. Even though she tried to maintain businesslike relationships, men sometimes made passes at her.

Some men deal with their discomfort at having a woman peer or manager by using sex to jockey women into position. Maggie's femininity, instead of being considered desirable, was used as a put-down. This confuses many women.

A little girl hears, "We don't want any girls on our team." It's rejection, because boys think girls are inferior. They try to keep girls in their place.

FEMININITY REJECTION

This is the opposite problem from the sexual put-down. You're upset when you're treated like one of the boys. You're in a double bind: If they're *not* making advances, you feel vaguely rejected.

A girl is often taught to use sex to get extra goodies if she can get away with it. If a sweet young thing is stopped for speeding, she's more likely to talk the policeman out of giving her a ticket if she acts feminine. A girl gets attention for being pretty. If a woman is treated in a professional, businesslike style, all these "fringe benefits" for being feminine are gone.

It may be that you've been taught that your whole identity is tied up with being a pretty woman or an attractive girl. When that's ignored, it's a blow to your identity and self-worth.

KNOWING THE IMPORTANCE OF RANK

In the army a general is obeyed and shown respect because of his rank. It doesn't matter that he beats his wife or kicks the dog. If you work under him you show him respect. In business your boss and your managers have rank. They may not necessarily have the type of personality or intellect *you* respect, but as long as you're working under them, you must show them respect. You may make the mistake of showing disrespect for a boss behind his back, unaware that it will get back to him and hurt your position with the company. Men know this is one of the rules of the game. It's an important one to learn. You may respect people because of how you feel about them, rather than for their positions.

This comes from being a lone star most of your life and not a team member. Men learn the importance of rank from games and from the military: The coach is respected because he's the coach; the general is respected because he's the general.

FRIENDS AND ASSOCIATES

You don't know how to use your social life to benefit your career position. You eat lunch with subordinates instead of trying to make friends with peers or superiors. You prefer people you "like." You forget that people are usually identified with the people they associate with. You fail to make alliances with those in the proper positions who can help you succeed in the company. You think it's wrong to become friendly with someone who can help you. It's "using" them.

"Using" people has a negative connotation for women. Women are called "social climbers," but not men. A man is "making contacts." The man who chooses friends who can help his career is considered prudent. Women don't know that business is done largely through informal contacts. These are the rules of the game. Men build themselves a support system at work. They know how to use their social lives to climb the ladder.

TEAMWORK

You want to be a star performer on your own, not make the *team* number one. You don't subordinate yourself in the company's interests. You are judgmental about your peers. You think you can only work with people you like or are comfortable with.

If this sounds like you, you are probably used to playing a solo act. Men know harmonious relations in a group are more important than being "right." They understand it's essential to work with the team as a unit. To not make ripples over inconsequential issues.

Little girls play one to one with people they like. They have a "best friend." They never get a chance to learn that you have to get along with everybody on the team to win. By playing on teams and in gangs, little boys learn to cooperate. They learn to put the good relations of the group first, to be tolerant, and to get along with other boys.

FAIR PLAY (IDEALISM)

You believe in justice. The world should be "fair." You have a romantic notion of the way things "ought to be." You see men as playing dirty. Since you expect justice, you're confused by the reality of the business world with its many seeming infractions.

Men have learned that in business, as in ball games, there's a premium on legal deceit. They are taught as boys that there are various kinds of permissible deceptions: bluffing, or certain things that can be done when the referee isn't looking. In the games girls play the rules are precise, and the best player is the one who follows them exactly. "I don't want to play with her, she cheats!" In girls' games, either you're cheating or you're not cheating. The rules are clear-cut.

In football a boy learns that the best plays, the most admirable ones, are the plays that stretch the rules as far as they will go without breaking them. A boy comes to see the rules as elastic, open to interpretation by the players. Boys often argue with each other about the rules. If they can get away with a play, it's okay. So a man develops an ability to bluff, or feign. You think it's "dishonest." He's being "clever." You're being "moral." He's being "practical." You ask, "Is it fair?" He asks, "Can I get away with it?"

You can see that there are many ways that one's conditioning helps or hinders life in the corporate world. At least a few of the situations I've just mentioned are probably familiar to you. The questionnaire in the next chapter will help you to pinpoint your particular problem areas.

BEHAVIOR QUESTIONNAIRE

3

When you go to your dentist or doctor you can usually point to the tooth or spot where it hurts, and that's usually where the trouble is. It's not so easy when you're hurting emotionally, when you're feeling disappointed, depressed, or frustrated with how things are going in your professional or personal life. If someone asks, "What's wrong?" or "What's the problem?" you can only come up with vague answers: "I'm just dissatisfied," "I feel like I'm in a rut"; "I'm not getting anywhere"; "Some days I don't even feel like going to the office"; "I don't like myself"; "Something's wrong but I don't know what."

Trying to help someone with those complaints is like trying to give directions to your house to a friend who has lost her way and can't give you any idea of where she's calling from. This is why we need a behavior questionnaire, so we can find out exactly where it is you are "calling from."

You develop certain patterns of behavior or ways of responding while you are growing up, and you carry these patterns into adulthood. In some situations they help you get what you want; in others they get in the way or hold you back. The trouble is, even when they work against you so that you're not getting what you want, you don't make the connection. You keep using the same styles of behavior and getting the same unsatisfying results. Naturally, you get discouraged. You may quit your job or end a relationship and start over again in a new setting. Nothing gets solved. Nothing changes, except the names of the players.

I want to help you to make the connections between what you're doing or not doing, and the results you're getting. But first we have to examine your behavior. How do you behave, or how do you think you'd behave or react in different situations and under different conditions? This is what you'll discover as you begin working on the questionnaire. As your behavioral picture develops you'll see clearly where your problem areas are.

Problem behaviors usually fall into two categories. There are those things you do too much of: "I talk too much"; "I defend myself too much"; "I try too hard to please people"; "I spend too much time trying to do even unimportant tasks perfectly"; "I'm too pushy." We call this a behavioral surplus. Then there are the things you don't do enough of: "I hold back from expressing myself"; "I don't take risks and I play it too safe"; "I don't like to give orders"; "I'm too quiet"; "I don't know how to say no"; "I work alone too much and not with other people." We call this a behavioral deficiency.

A problem in an area such as assertiveness ("I don't know how to say no") might simply mean that you're lacking skills in that department, and assertiveness training may be all you'll need to correct the deficiency. A surplus behavior ("I talk too much") may call for monitoring or checking yourself, and then some practical instruction as to what's appropriate and what isn't in particular situations.

In most cases, however, problem behaviors don't get solved that easily. You usually have to do more than just learn a new skill or increase your self-awareness. That's because bad habits, which is what problem behaviors are, have been with you for a long time. Think for a moment of one of your own. How long, without being aware of it, have you been doing it? Maybe it served a purpose, and maybe it still does. You might ask what purpose could possibly be served by habits such as talking too much and driving people up the wall; or by trying so hard to do things perfectly that you only get half as many things accomplished; or by not being assertive and hating yourself afterwards because you let someone take advantage of you. Well, habits such as these may help you feel a little less uncomfortable in a tense situation—for the moment. In the long run, though, you end up feeling less confident, and your self-worth drops lower.

If you feel incompetent or out of place in a particular social situation, you may actually be feeling anxious. Anxiety is nearly always involved in the development of a problem behavior. For example, if confrontation makes you uneasy or anxious, then being unassertive is a good way to avoid both confrontation and anxiety. Are you chattering compulsively with a male executive because you are painfully uncomfortable with gaps of silence in the conversation or because you're anxious about his opinion of you? Are you so worried or anxious about people not liking you that you avoid positions where you may have to give them orders? Are you so fearful of criticism that you try to avoid it by being "perfect"? Do you fear disapproval so much that you play it safe by never taking risks?

This gives you some idea of how anxiety or fears can lead to patterns of behavior that work *against,* not *for* you. It's important to see the connection, and to recognize the anxieties involved in your problem behaviors. When you learn how to get rid of underlying fears and reduce your anxieties, you'll feel more relaxed in social and business situations that once were stressful to you. With the tension gone you'll feel comfortable with yourself and others. In cases where new behavioral skills are called for, you'll have no trouble learning and practicing them when you have eliminated most of the anxiety.

In the chapters that follow I will be describing techniques I use to rid people of unnecessary fears and help them control anxiety. I will show you how you can use them to make yourself less sensitive to criticism, disapproval, and rejection; less uptight with authority figures and bosses or in social situations; less fearful of making mistakes or taking risks; and more assertive.

Remember, these patterns of behavior and ways of behaving—habits—have been *learned* over a long period of time. You've gotten used to them and, until now, you've accepted the way your life has been limited by them. Do you use statements such as "That just happens to be the way I am"; "I'm not the kind of person who can . . ."? As a woman, you may not even have seen them as limitations, but simply accepted the distorted notion that "That's the way I *should* be."

It's the purpose of this book to show you how inappropriate or nonproductive behaviors can be *unlearned* and replaced with alternative, positive ones. Of course, no book can be a substitute for personal therapy. Complex problems or severe disorders require treatment by a competent psychologist or psychiatrist.

Now get a pencil so you can score yourself on the following behavior questionnaire and see what *your* behavioral profile looks like.

BEHAVIOR QUESTIONNAIRE

Circle the number that comes closest to representing your response, as follows:

(1) never
(2) rarely

(3) sometimes
(4) a great deal
(5) always

A. *SEXUALITY*

1. Do you wear sexy clothes to the office?   1 2 3 4 5
2. When the going gets tough do you use seductiveness to get your way?   1 2 3 4 5
3. Do you find it disturbing when men treat you like "one of the boys"?   1 2 3 4 5
4. Do you encourage men to act protectively toward you?   1 2 3 4 5
5. Do you expect men to open doors or hold seats for you?   1 2 3 4 5
6. When you feel especially pretty, or have made a special effort to look attractive, are you bothered when no one notices?   1 2 3 4 5
7. When you are among a group of male colleagues, are you annoyed when their attention is suddenly focused on a woman making an obvious display of feminine charm?   1 2 3 4 5

(Add the circled numbers) *Total score* A._____

B. *NURTURING*

1. Do you encourage people to come to you with their problems?   1 2 3 4 5
2. Do you offer to do errands for others at the office?   1 2 3 4 5
3. Does preparing coffee for your boss or colleagues make you feel good?   1 2 3 4 5
4. Do you suggest or offer home remedies when people tell you their medical problems?   1 2 3 4 5
5. Do you keep a supply of aspirin and Band-

Aids in your desk for the use of co-work-
ers?   1 2 3 4 5
6. Do you volunteer for nonwork-related duties?   1 2 3 4 5
7. Do you play down your accomplishments
or successes at work to your husband or
boyfriend as a way of keeping them hap-
py?   1 2 3 4 5

Total score B._____

C. ORGANIZATION

1. Do you have to be reminded by others of
important appointments?   1 2 3 4 5
2. Do you arrive late for appointments?   1 2 3 4 5
3. Is it difficult for you to locate files or ref-
erences when you're in a hurry?   1 2 3 4 5
4. Do you remember important points you
wished to raise at a meeting only after
the meeting has ended?   1 2 3 4 5
5. Is it difficult for you to clarify priorities
among your work load during the course
of the day?   1 2 3 4 5
6. Is getting out of the house in the morning
especially time consuming because of mis-
placed articles of clothing, keys, change,
etc.?   1 2 3 4 5
7. Do you arrive at airports, train or bus sta-
tions with barely a minute to spare?   1 2 3 4 5

Total score C:_____

D. PASSIVITY

1. In a restaurant do you let your companion
order for you?   1 2 3 4 5
2. Do you avoid taking the initiative in
changing things you don't like?   1 2 3 4 5

3. Do you attribute important changes in your life or career to chance rather than to your own efforts?   1 2 3 4 5

4. In an emergency situation do you tend to step aside and let someone else take over? 1 2 3 4 5

5. If your initial efforts at solving a problem fail, do you look to others for help?   1 2 3 4 5

6. If there's a position available that you would like, do you hesitate to make the effort to acquire the necessary skills to be selected?   1 2 3 4 5

7. On a vacation trip, do you prefer to have someone else plan your itinerary rather than do it yourself?   1 2 3 4 5

Total score D:_____

E. *PERFECTIONISM*

1. Does it upset you when a job you've done falls slightly below your standards?   1 2 3 4 5

2. If you notice a minor flaw in a paper or report you've already submitted, or become aware of an inaccurate remark you made in an earlier conversation, does it ruin your day?   1 2 3 4 5

3. When you regard a colleague's completed work that he or she is satisfied with, do you ever think, "I wouldn't be satisfied with those results?"   1 2 3 4 5

4. Do you get impatient when you watch someone doing a job that you believe you could do better?   1 2 3 4 5

5. Do you have difficulty making deadlines because you devote a great deal of time to details?   1 2 3 4 5

6. Do you regard yourself as a failure when

you don't come out in first place, or are
judged the best?   1 2 3 4 5
7. When learning a new skill, do you lose
interest and quit if, by your standards,
you aren't doing well?   1 2 3 4 5

Total score E:_____

Imagine yourself in the following hypothetical situations.
Then answer the questions in terms of how likely or unlikely it
would be that you would react in the way suggested. Rate
yourself on the following scale:

(1) definitely no
(2) not likely
(3) 50/50 possibility
(4) likely
(5) definitely yes

F. *TEAMWORK*
1. Your best ideas have been used successfully by a sales promotion team you've been
working with. You receive no individual
recognition but your team is commended.
Would you be dissatisfied?   1 2 3 4 5
2. While you and your boss are entertaining
a buyer, the matter of a past order mix-up
is discussed. While it was actually your
boss's fault at the time, it is now made to
look as if it were yours. Would you try to
set the record straight by pointing out his
mistake in front of the buyer?   1 2 3 4 5
3. You learn that someone you personally
dislike is joining a group project with you.
Would it be *difficult* for you to put your
differences aside and collaborate with

him/her for the benefit of the project?   1 2 3 4 5
4. Your department wins an award for a promotional idea based entirely upon one of
your suggestions. Would you feel let down
if you were not singled out for credit?   1 2 3 4 5
5. Some of the members of a sales team
you've been working with have been goof-
ing off. The group is called before the director. Would you do your best to exoner-
ate yourself individually rather than defend the group?   1 2 3 4 5
6. You are privy to information that would
bring credit to your department but none
to you individually. Would you withhold
it?   1 2 3 4 5
7. You are asked to share and coordinate
your ideas with a group of out-of-town
sales reps new in the field. Would you be
reluctant to disclose your best ideas?   1 2 3 4 5

Total score F:_____

G. *RISK TAKING*

Now use the same scale to rate yourself on how likely or
unlikely it is that you would:
1. Avoid taking on added responsibilities
when offered?   1 2 3 4 5
2. Refuse an assignment when you know that
others have failed at it?   1 2 3 4 5
3. Stay with a comfortable and secure position where there is no chance of advancement, rather than accept a new one with
potential for personal advancement with
a company whose future is promising but
uncertain?   1 2 3 4 5
4. Hesitate about relocating to the East or

West Coast for a better paying and higher
level executive position with a different
company?   1 2 3 4 5
5. Turn down an assignment out of town,
where you must work with a group of men
known to be provincial or sexist in their
thinking?   1 2 3 4 5
6. In the absence of your boss *avoid* making
a critical decision that could, depending
on the outcome, earn you either praise or
criticism from the top?   1 2 3 4 5
7. Be reluctant to submit a constructive
though critical report you had written to
the company's president outlining ways to
improve your department's efficiency?   1 2 3 4 5
Total score G:_____

H. *COMPETITIVENESS*

How likely or unlikely is it that you would:
1. Not take a job where promotions depended
on competing with your peers?   1 2 3 4 5
2. Give up when your work was compared
unfavorably to that of others, as opposed
to trying harder?   1 2 3 4 5
3. Hold back from presenting your ideas at
a meeting for fear they would not be as
valuable as others?   1 2 3 4 5
4. Be discouraged when a new and younger
employee, with a more diversified background than you, is brought in to your
department, as opposed to being motivated
to expand your own background?   1 2 3 4 5
5. Be more comfortable dating a man you
liked whom not many other women were
interested in, rather than a man you liked

more and knew other women were competing for. 1 2 3 4 5

6. Change careers or professions because of the amount of competition in that particular field? 1 2 3 4 5

7. Choose to watch rather than participate in a competitive game of tennis (Ping-Pong, racquet ball, etc.)? 1 2 3 4 5

Total Score H._____

I. *ASSERTIVENESS*

How easy or difficult would it be for you to handle the following situations? Rate yourself as follows:

(1) very easy
(2) easy
(3) not so easy
(4) quite difficult
(5) extremely difficult

1. Tell someone about to light a cigarette that you would like them not to smoke. 1 2 3 4 5

2. Maintain eye contact while you are in conversation with another person. 1 2 3 4 5

3. Accept a compliment from your boss. 1 2 3 4 5

4. Complain to your boss when you feel you've been treated unfairly. 1 2 3 4 5

5. Say no to a friend or co-worker who asked to borrow money or some personal item of yours. 1 2 3 4 5

6. Express your annoyance to a friend who has disappointed you. 1 2 3 4 5

7. Disagree with your boss over an issue you have very strong feelings about. 1 2 3 4 5

Total score I:_____

J. *GIVING ORDERS*
How easy or difficult would it be for you to:

1. Tell a waiter you want special service because you are in a hurry to meet an appointment?   1 2 3 4 5
2. Tell the mail room clerk to wrap a book for you for mailing to a friend?   1 2 3 4 5
3. Tell the file clerk to come in an hour early to do a special job for you?   1 2 3 4 5
4. Tell a secretary to make an airline and hotel reservation for you?   1 2 3 4 5
5. Tell a cab driver to drive slower or faster?   1 2 3 4 5
6. Tell a typist to retype a letter because of a mistake you had made in your original instructions?   1 2 3 4 5
7. Tell the office cleaning lady to wash out your waste basket or clean under your desk?   1 2 3 4 5

Total score J:_____

Try to imagine how uncomfortable, upset, or bothered you would be under the following circumstances. Then rate yourself as follows:

(1) not at all upset
(2) slightly upset
(3) moderately upset
(4) very upset
(5) extremely upset

K. *CRITICISM*

1. Your report is returned with a notation by your boss that it is not thorough enough.   1 2 3 4 5

2. A co-worker comments negatively on
your new hair style.   1 2 3 4 5
3. Your boyfriend or husband complains of
the untidy condition of your room or
desk.   1 2 3 4 5
4. A colleague tells you the question you
raised at the board or sales meeting was
off target.   1 2 3 4 5
5. You overhear a group of subordinates
refer to you as a slave driver.   1 2 3 4 5
6. You hear from a friend that a business
associate whom you respect remarked
that you tend to be overtalkative at
times.   1 2 3 4 5
7. A friend comments that you are putting
on weight.   1 2 3 4 5

Total score K:_____

L. *REJECTION*

1. You've left three telephone messages with
a department head and he still fails to return your call.   1 2 3 4 5
2. You enter a restaurant alone and several
male associates see you but do not ask you
to join their table.   1 2 3 4 5
3. The promotion you had expected doesn't
come through.   1 2 3 4 5
4. A competitor wins the order from a buyer
you had been soliciting for three months. 1 2 3 4 5
5. The doorman ignores you as he rushes to
open the door of a taxi pulling up with
another tenant.   1 2 3 4 5
6. A larger office that you had expected to
be moved to, pending its availability, is
given to a co-worker with less seniority. 1 2 3 4 5

7. On a business trip you are bumped from
   your scheduled flight to Chicago and your
   place is given to a VIP.   1 2 3 4 5
                                   Total score L:_____

M. *PUBLIC SPEAKING*
1. Playing a role in an amateur drama production.   1 2 3 4 5
2. Asking a question from your seat in a
   classroom of thirty adult students.   1 2 3 4 5
3. Presenting a new idea during a meeting
   of your colleagues.   1 2 3 4 5
4. Reading a prepared statement to a group
   of associates that includes the head of
   your department and your boss.   1 2 3 4 5
5. Appearing on a radio talk show.   1 2 3 4 5
6. On a crowded bus, calling out to the driver when he reaches your stop and fails to
   stop.   1 2 3 4 5
7. Being approached on the street by a rov-
   ing T.V. newsperson and camera crew,
   and asked to express your opinion on a
   current political issue.   1 2 3 4 5
                                   Total score M:_____

N. *AUTHORITY FIGURES*
1. At a cocktail party you are introduced to
   the chairman of the board, who asks you
   about your department's activities.   1 2 3 4 5
2. You are given a message that your boss
   wants you in his office immediately.   1 2 3 4 5
3. You do not understand the diagnosis your
   doctor has given you and must ask him to
   explain your problem to you more clearly.   1 2 3 4 5

4. Your doorbell rings. You answer it and
   find a policeman there.   1 2 3 4 5
5. The boss enters your office while you are
   on the phone talking to a girl friend.   1 2 3 4 5
6. After you have entered an exclusive res-
   taurant the maître d' informs you in a
   cold manner that you cannot be seated
   unaccompanied.   1 2 3 4 5
7. As you are about to step into a cab on a
   rainy day, your company's president runs
   over and asks if you would mind him rid-
   ing uptown with you.   1 2 3 4 5

Total score N:_____

KEY TO THE BEHAVIOR QUESTIONNAIRE

Add up your scores for each problem category. Here is the key
for interpreting your results.

Over but	Under	
7	14	Definitely no problems in this area. You seem to be handling these situations well.
15	21	You can probably do even better, once you've learned how to use the self-help methods described in the chapter that follows.
22	28	Looks like you have some problems here. Familiarize yourself with the techniques in Chapter Four and read in particular the chapter dealing with your problem.
29	35	You definitely need help here. Learn the techniques in Chapter Four so you can apply them to your problem.

WORKING ON YOUR PARTICULAR PROBLEM

A. Sexuality

A problem with the misuse of sex calls for a look at your personal beliefs. You may need to check your priorities. For example, if getting rewarded for being a desirable female is at the top of your list, you may be depending too much on feminine wiles to get what you want, or you may be underestimating your other assets. Now may be a good time to evaluate your abilities and assets realistically. If doing without your accustomed dose of male attentiveness is painful, you can learn some techniques that will make you less anxious in situations where your womanliness goes unnoticed. You can catch yourself when you are playing it coy or being manipulative, and try to play it straight. You can also learn alternative ways of behaving, through the use of imagery techniques, as described in Chapter Four.

If misusing sex is a particular problem for you, pay special attention to the chapter "Sex in the Office."

B. Nurturing

Have you accepted the belief that because you are a woman, yours is a nurturing role? You may believe that nothing is more important than being liked by everyone, and think that it's what you do for them, not how you are as a person, that determines how much people will like you. If fear of not being liked underlies your mothering of others, you can learn techniques that will cause you not to be anxious when confronted with rejection or disapproval. You also may want to check out and change some of the things you've been saying to yourself about how helpless a certain person may be, and how he or she can't manage without you. If it's just not your habit to say no, you may also need some assertiveness training. Then you can start to turn down requests and resist volunteering in imaginary scenes, after which you can do the same in actual situations. This technique, which is called behavior rehearsal, is described in the following chapter.

You will also find it helpful to study carefully Chapter Twelve, "Nurturing," as well as Chapter Five, "Assertiveness."

C. Organization

If you have a problem in this area it's probably a simple matter of a behavioral deficiency: You've just never learned the basic skills of putting the things in your life in order. Your desk may be a good place to start. Develop the habit of making lists, working out time schedules and identifying priorities. You'll learn fastest by observing the person in your office who accomplishes the most with the least effort and whose desk appears orderly and uncluttered. How does she do things? And how can you apply what you observe to your work?

D. Passivity

Do you still believe that the good things in life just "happen"; that your rewards will arrive—unsolicited and magically—by special messenger? All good things do not come to those who wait, unless your name is Cinderella and your godmother is a fairy. Assertiveness training will teach you to *ask* for what you want, and turn down what you don't want. Notice someone who is actively involved in directing the course of her life, someone in control, going after and getting what she wants in a positive and constructive way. A good model, a woman you admire, is your best teacher. You can imagine yourself filling that role in different situations. You can practice taking a more active and assertive role in actual situations, starting small and gradually working up to more important things.

If passivity is a problem for you, Chapter Eight will be particularly helpful.

E. *Perfectionism*

If you're a perfectionist you're probably struggling along with a set of mistaken beliefs, such as "Unless I do everything perfectly, I'm a failure"; "So long as I'm perfect I'll never be criticized and will be approved of and loved." It's time you examined these irrational beliefs and changed them. Don't be too hard on yourself. Start by spending less time on projects, deliberately letting reports or papers leave your desk with tiny flaws only you would be aware of. With relaxation techniques you can cut down on the stress you subject yourself to. You will function *better* under less tension, and get more done in the same period of time. Unimportant things don't require the same amount of time and energy as important things. You can learn to make the distinction. If you have a tendency to dwell on your minor errors, going over and over in your head what you *could* or *should* have done—what is called *ruminating*—then you can use a technique called thought-stopping. Chapter Thirteen, "Being a Perfectionist," will be especially useful to you.

F. *Teamwork*

A problem with teamwork may be just one of habit. You're accustomed to performing solo, and you've learned to enjoy the applause without having to share it. Learning to be part of a group, taking special pride in that group identity, and sharing the larger rewards will take a little adjusting. If you find it painful not to get individual attention for your efforts, some of the techniques explained in the following chapter can make it easier for you. The gratification you will enjoy from being part of a winning team and the enthusiasm that becomes contagious among team members may pleasantly surprise you.

You may want to study carefully Chapter Fourteen, "Competition and Teamwork."

G. Risk Taking

You may be playing it too safe, either out of habit or out of fear. Tune in on the messages you're giving to yourself—your self-talk—and you will become more aware of how you're frightening yourself. You can learn to separate *real* risks from *imaginary* ones, and to weigh the realistic risks and evaluate the situation and yourself. For example, if you're applying for a new job, check your skills; by being prepared you will minimize risks in a new position. Underlying the fear of taking risks are the fears of failing, of being criticized, or of being rejected. Some of the techniques explained in the following chapter will help you conquer these anxieties and fears. You can create images of yourself enjoying the challenge and stimulation of stepping out of the familiar and secure places you're so comfortable in—and of winning. You can use a technique called thought-stopping if your mind fills up with images of failure and rejection whenever the opportunity to take a risk comes up.

If you have a problem with risk taking, Chapter Seven will give you more information about how to handle risks successfully.

H. Competitiveness

If you are avoiding competition, you are, like many women who avoid taking risks, playing it safe. Similar fears may be involved: fear of failing, of losing, and the more personal fear of being disliked. You can reduce those fears with several techniques explained in the next chapter. You can examine what you are saying to yourself—your self-talk—for "disaster messages." Persistent negative thoughts may require the technique called thought-stopping. Probably you will benefit by a realistic evaluation of your strengths and weaknesses. Some assertiveness training may also help.

For more information read Chapter Fourteen, "Competition and Teamwork."

I. Assertiveness

If you're unassertive in a variety of situations you might consider joining an assertiveness training workshop. In addition, a good role model—a woman executive you admire—can teach you a great deal. If, however, the mere thought of asserting yourself shakes you up, you will need to use some of the techniques to reduce anxiety about criticism and rejection that are explained in the next chapter. Learning assertive skills won't help if you are so highly anxious that you can't put them into practice.

Chapters Five and Six will tell you more about assertiveness.

J. Giving Orders

This behavior may be totally foreign to you. You can begin by watching how others do it. Choose your model from among the more effective and popular women executives around you. Then you can do a lot of practicing, or role rehearsal, in your imagination, before you try role rehearsal in real life. Start with people and situations that are the least threatening, and gradually work up to those that are more demanding.

You will also find it useful to study carefully the chapters on assertiveness.

K. Criticism

The best buffer against criticism is exposure. In the chapter that follows you will learn how to decrease your anxiety about criticism by using imagery. If you carry someone's critical remark around with you all day and take it to bed with you at night, you can practice the thought-stopping technique. If a criticism of you is valid, you may learn something by asking for more constructive feedback.

You will benefit by reading carefully Chapter Ten, "Criticism and Rejection." Also review the rules for good communication in the chapters on assertiveness.

L. Rejection

Bothered by rejection? Join the club. No one likes to be rejected. You can make it much worse, though, if you allow it to feed every negative thought you have about yourself and probably the world. You can learn to tune in on these destructive messages you give yourself, and thereby get a better perspective on the situation and on yourself. If you persist in using negative thoughts, then you'll need to use thought-stopping. Humanizing the source of the rejection also helps put the situation in proper perspective and makes it less upsetting. If you're still extremely sensitive to rejection, you can learn the techniques to reduce anxiety that are described in the next chapter.

You will want to read Chapter Ten, "Criticism and Rejection," for more information.

M. Public Speaking

Some anxiety here, like stage fright, is natural. You can practice relaxation training, as outlined in the next chapter. Also valuable is a technique called role rehearsal in imagery. If you're new at public speaking, there may be some skills to learn, such as organization of material, researching subject matter, preparing cue cards, voice control, timing, and so on. Live role rehearsal before small groups and working up to larger groups and more intimidating audiences will shape your behavior and build confidence. Check your self-talk for disaster messages. If a number of "But what if?" questions persist in your head, use the thought-stopping technique.

N. Authority Figures

Seeing the people you let intimidate you in a different light—humanizing them—will take much of their power away. Assertiveness training can teach you how to respond appropriately and maintain your dignity. If necessary you can put the most fearful authority figures in your life in imaginary situations and decrease your anxiety about them by using a technique called gradual painless exposure (GPE), which is explained in the next chapter.

You will benefit by giving Chapter Eleven, "Authority Figures," special attention.

THE TECHNIQUES
EXPLAINED

4

Since I will be showing you how to learn new ways of behaving and new ways to respond emotionally to certain situations, I think you will find it useful to understand how a person learns to behave the way he or she does.

Much of what we know about learning and conditioning has come to us from the laboratories of behavioral scientists. Researchers have been able to use human and animal studies to draw some interesting conclusions about conditioning. They've discovered that conditioning occurs in two different ways.

The first theory was formulated by the famous Russian physiologist Ivan Pavlov, in his well-known experiments with dogs. Pavlov found he could get a hungry dog to salivate just by ringing a bell. He first had to train the dog to make the connection between the bell and the food. He did this by consistently repeating, one after the other, the bell first, followed by the food.

In another well-known experiment, a healthy child was conditioned to be afraid of a white rabbit and even white furry objects that looked like rabbits. The experimenter used a white rabbit that had been the child's favorite pet. Every time the rabbit was placed in the child's crib, the experimenter made a loud, startling noise behind the child, out of his sight. The little boy recoiled from the rabbit in fear, and hid under a blanket, crying. After this sequence was repeated a number of times, first the rabbit, then the frightening noise, it soon happened that whenever the child saw the rabbit, or a similar furry object, he showed the same fear, even when the noise didn't follow.

In both these experiments a normal, involuntary response to food or a sudden loud noise, became strongly connected to a totally unrelated cue, like a bell or rabbit, only because of repeated association.

You may not realize how much of what you have learned during your life is the result of this type of association or conditioning. There are numerous ways in which you respond almost automatically—without thinking—to certain everyday signals. The traffic light turns green, and you step off the curb to cross the street. If you're driving, your foot automatically lifts off the accelerator and your pulse may quicken at the sound of a police siren. If you're at home alone on a Saturday night, wishing you had a date, you jump up and maybe your heart skips a beat at the sound of your telephone ringing. These are all reactions—some pleasant, some unpleasant— that you have learned through their repeated association with different signals in your environment.

Here's an example of how an association, or conditioned reaction, can carry over into other areas of our lives: The stern voice of her father calling, "Elizabeth!" was enough to start Beth's heart bounding rapidly, make her palms moist, and her knees shaky. Early in her childhood Beth had learned that when her father called her "Elizabeth" something unpleasant was bound to follow. Her conditioning was so strong that for the first three weeks on her new job, whenever she heard her boss shout, "Elizabeth!" the same anxiety was triggered in her body, and she found herself trembling without knowing why.

Sometimes an upsetting event only has to occur once or twice in order for a fear to develop. When Joyce was vacationing in Florida five years ago she was stopped for speeding. The police kept her in a stuffy police station for almost six hours, and fined her a hundred dollars. She was frightened, and her vacation was ruined. A year later she was caught speeding again on the New England Thruway by a motorcycle cop. Today, at the first sight of any motorcycle in her rearview mirror, Joyce's foot lifts automatically off the gas pedal, her pulse races, her mouth goes dry—until the rider passes her or she's able to make sure it's not a policeman.

Some learned responses last longer than others. After Beth had worked with her new boss for a while, she discovered that what followed his calling "Elizabeth!" was nothing at all like what happened when her father did it. Eventually she was no longer afraid to hear "Elizabeth!" Her original fear gradually weakened. But if her boss had been harsh or intimidating— anything like her father was when he was angry—the association would have been strengthened, and hearing "Elizabeth!" would have continued to cause Beth anxiety.

As you may have noticed, this type of conditioning deals with emotional reactions and physiological reactions. Psychologists refer to it as *Pavlovian*, or *classical, conditioning*.

The second type of conditioning deals with how we learn to behave in different ways as a result of how others respond to our actions or behaviors, or according to the kind of feedback we get from our environment. B. F. Skinner, who calls it *operant conditioning*, has stated the underlying principle very simply: *All behavior is shaped by its consequences*. You are more likely to repeat something that gets good results or some kind of reward. And you are less likely to repeat any behavior that is punished or gets unpleasant results.

Why, then, do some people—children, for instance— have "bad" behavior? Because often a child's troublesome behavior is being rewarded, unknowingly, by the parent. Little Susie whines and pouts because she's learned that it's a sure way to get her mother to give her an ice-cream cone to quiet her down and bring peace to the household. Susie is rewarded for whining. She learns that this is a good way to get what she wants. The next time she wants ice cream, or any other goodie, she will probably whine and pout again. But, if mom ignores Susie when she whines and cries, that is, gives her "time out" until her tantrum is over, Susie would soon learn that whining and crying don't work. If her mom gives her ice cream only when Susie behaves in a pleasant or appropriate manner, then Susie will learn that pleasant behavior, not whining behavior, is what will get her what she wants, and she'll be more likely to behave that way again.

What if mom and all the other adults in the family keep reinforcing the whining behavior by unintentionally respond- ing or rewarding Susie for whining and crying? Susie may reach adolescence believing that the best way to get what she wants is to passively pout, sulk, or be on the edge of tears. The hurt, little-girl voice begging for just one more special favor will be found irresistible by some men. But Susie will be at a great disadvantage in the business world if she expects these tactics to help her there.

Susie's case shows just one way behavior can be learned and then strengthened because it keeps getting positive results. It also shows how a strategy that works well in one area of a person's life can create serious problems when it occurs in another area. Being helpless and dependent may make little girls more "appealing" to adults, but if enough adults reward them for it, helplessness and dependency eventually become a style of behavior. The trouble is, these ways of behaving will not be effective in a competitive environment.

Now we will look at a number of techniques that behavior therapists have developed to help people unlearn certain learned responses and change their behavior. These techniques are based on the two kinds of learning you just read about. They are not difficult to learn; chances are you are already using some of them in your everyday life, although you may not be aware of it.

Many of these techniques rely upon the power of mental imagery. You may not realize it, but you are constantly creating or affirming images in your mind, as you think or as you go about your daily activities. As you drive to the supermarket or walk to the bus stop, the streets you cross, the houses or stores you pass—all so familiar to you—are images recorded in your memory. You see everything in its usual place, that is, according to your preset mental image. A detour, or something out of place, may slow you momentarily as you adjust your image or record a new one.

We plan and often think in images. We create images or fantasies of future situations, and, of course, we create—with the help of others—our own self-images. When Louise tells Judy, "I just *know* I'm going to be nervous at the meeting tomorrow, I can see myself making a perfect fool of myself," she is creating a negative image in her mind of that future situation. She actually does "see" herself in her mind's eye in the calamitous position she describes. Worst of all, she is programming herself for failure.

"I *know* I'm not going to enjoy myself at the party tonight," Martha tells her roommate, while she conjures up pictures in her mind of looking unattractive, acting awkward, and being unsociable. She will very likely find herself acting out that picture at the party, fulfilling that gloomy picture she has already rehearsed in her mind.

A survey of gymnasts showed that those who were consistently successful had positive expectations, that is, "saw" themselves performing well before a competition. Those who did poorly admitted that just before performing they had thoughts or images of themselves slipping on a dismount or at some other critical spot in their routine.

Images, our own private ones or those of others projected on a movie or TV screen, strongly influence how we see ourselves and how we act with others. Spend two hours watching and identifying with your favorite star as she dominates the screen, and see if you don't leave the theater walking, speaking, or gesturing in ways just a little different from your usual style.

After several people have told you how fabulous you look when you've returned from a vacation, the image you form of yourself becomes more positive and you feel and act with greater confidence. The trouble is, if you have let yourself become too dependent upon such feedback to shape the image you carry of yourself in your mind, you don't have much control over how you feel about yourself. I'm going to show you how to get more control by learning to take an active role in shaping those self-images.

But before you practice the imagery techniques I describe, it's important you first learn how to relax your mind and your body as fully as possible. The best method I know for achieving a deep state of physical and mental relaxation is through deep muscle relaxation exercises. Through these exercises you'll discover and enjoy a calmness and serenity you may not have thought possible. This is the ideal state to be in when you use many of the techniques that follow and, as you will see later, is an essential part of *gradual painless exposure* (GPE). Learning to relax is a skill that takes practice but is well worth the effort. It can help you to reduce stress in all areas of your life.

Here's how you can practice deep muscle relaxation and avoid stress without resorting to drugs or other artificial means.

DEEP MUSCLE RELAXATION

Most people don't realize that relaxing a muscle is an activity, just as tensing a muscle is an activity. These exercises train you by tensing and then *actively* relaxing different muscle groups throughout your body. You should pay particular attention to the *difference* between the feeling of tension and the feeling of relaxation as you do the exercises. When you increase your awareness of that difference then relaxation will become a habit. You won't allow tension to build up in your body.

The best place to practice relaxation exercises is in a comfortable arm chair or recliner, or sitting slouched on a sofa. Lying in bed gives you less freedom of movement, and is too closely associated with sleeping. Take the phone off the hook and ask your family not to disturb you for a while. Take off your bracelets, shoes, or any tight clothing that may interfere with your being comfortable. A good idea, if you have a tape recorder, is to tape the instructions that follow, so you can play them back to yourself while you practice them with your eyes closed. Record them slowly, using a low, calm voice.

Begin by taking a very deep breath, hold it for three or four seconds, then exhale slowly, all the way out, pushing the last bit of breath out by contracting your stomach muscles. Do that once more, then go on breathing normally and easily, and allow your eyes to close. Now, clench your fists as tightly as you can. Notice where you feel tension in the back of your hands and the upper part of your forearms. Hold for about five seconds, then gradually, slowly, release the tension, letting your hands open and the fingers relax. Notice the difference in feeling in your hands and forearms. Do that once more. Tense both fists, study the tension for five seconds, then allow the tension to give way as you deliberately relax your hands and forearm muscles.

Leave your arms resting where they are and just bend your

hands back at the wrists so that your fingers are pointing up at the ceiling. Bend them back as far as you can so that you can feel the tension running up from your wrists through your forearms. Focus on that tension for five seconds, then, little by little, actively release those muscles as you would release a taut rubber band and allow it to go slack. Let it go more . . . more . . . more . . . until your hands are totally limp and relaxed. Feel the tingling sensation in your arms as the muscles relax and the tension eases. Then try to relax your arms just a little bit more. Repeat that. Now bend both arms at the elbows and tense your biceps, the muscles of the upper arms, the way you did as a child when you were challenged to "make a muscle." Hold and feel the muscles tighten. Now let your arms come down slowly and notice the tension gradually disappear as you allow your arms to settle and the muscles go limp. Good.

Now shrug your shoulders real hard as if you were trying to make them meet, and at the same time bend your head back as far as you can. Study the tensions you've created in the back of your neck and across your upper back. Hold for five seconds. . . . Now let your shoulders collapse and bring your head back to a normal resting position. Roll it from side to side until it rests comfortably. Imagine tension melting away from your shoulders just as you've seen snow melting on a white picket fence under a bright sun in winter. Do that once more. Head back, shoulders tensed, hold . . . and relax. Notice the difference between the sensations of tension and relaxation. Notice how much more relaxed your shoulders, arms, and hands feel compared to the rest of your body. Continue breathing calmly and deeply.

Next, wrinkle your forehead by raising your eyebrows as far as you can. Hold. . . . Now do the opposite by pulling your eyebrows down into a severe frown, and hold that. And now relax your brow and feel your forehead go smooth as all the lines of tension disappear from its surface. Now close your eyes very tightly, wrinkle up your nose, and with your jaw clamped shut draw the corners of your mouth all the way back so you can feel your cheeks tighten. Hold for five seconds . . . then relax. Feel all the tension drain away from your facial and jaw muscles. Very good.

Next, you're going to tense and relax your chest muscles. Take a deep breath, hold it, and with your arms bent, press the palms of your hands together. Hold. . . . Study the tension in the pectoral muscles. And now exhale and relax. Breathe deeply and comfortably. Now pretend someone is about to hit you in the stomach with their fist, and make your abdominal muscles as hard as you can. Hold that . . . And now relax your stomach muscles. Let them go completely. Think of a Buddha's stomach, rolls of flesh just hanging out, and let your stomach become just as relaxed.

Now stretch your legs out in front of you. Make them as straight and as stiff as you can, feet and toes pointing downward. Feel the tension in your thighs and calf muscles, in your ankles and the arches of both feet. Hold that for five seconds. . . . Now slowly lower your legs until your feet are resting on the floor, and feel all the muscles in your upper and lower legs letting go, more and more. Imagine those large and small muscles becoming soft and relaxed so that your legs feel as if they belonged to a rag doll. Continue breathing easily and deeply.

Now I want you take a few more minutes to allow the soothing sensations of deep muscle relaxation to spread even more deeply throughout your body. Imagine a gentle ripple of a wave of relaxation slowly moving over your scalp and forehead, easing away all tension in its path. You feel it caressing the tiny muscles in the outer corners of your eyes, down your cheeks, and around your jaw and mouth. You can feel your jaw loosening up a bit more as your mouth parts ever so slightly. Imagine your face and forehead so smooth now, as all lines of tension slowly dissolve away.

The ripple of relaxation continues down into your neck, spreads across your chest, shoulders, and back. You are letting go more and more now, and you are breathing very deeply and comfortably. And now you become aware of the same warm, relaxing sensations beginning at your fingertips, moving into the muscles of your palms, across the back of your hands and wrists. Your hands are perfectly limp now, and the same heavy feeling moves into your forearms and upper arms, so that the upper part of your body is feeling more and more relaxed. And now you can feel the muscles of your lower back releasing any remaining tension that might be there, as the ripple of relaxation soaks in, melting it away. Your buttocks muscles are letting go now, more and more, the large muscles of your thighs are loose and limp. The pleasant, magical wave of relaxation seeps down now into the muscles of your calves, into your ankles, the arches of your feet, and your toes. Your entire body is bathed in a comforting warmth of deep muscle relaxation. You feel beautifully calm and relaxed.

You are feeling very calm and quiet. Allow your body to sink now deeper, deeper, down . . . down into a deeper state of relaxation. Your limbs feel very heavy, you are so deliciously relaxed. You can imagine floating on a boat or on a cloud, drifting lazily along. Now see a pleasant, peaceful scene where you would like to be, and put yourself there now. Make it a private, special place; maybe it's somewhere you have been before, a scene where you always had good feelings. Create all the details in your imagination: the time, the season, all the colors, sounds, and smells. Imagine people there, if you want any, and see yourself there too. Perhaps you are resting peacefully in beautiful woods or along a lake or at the seashore. Now savor the scene in your imagination, and enjoy the good feeling it gives you. Remember this place, and when any anxiety prevents you from achieving relaxation, use this scene as a special calm place to go back to.

Practice the relaxation exercise at least once a day, and

twice if possible. Soon you will be able to let go of tension and slip into a comfortable, perfectly relaxed state. You may need to practice for a week or more before you can reach a relaxed state quickly and easily. Some people find it helpful to imagine the relaxation as a wave that soaks them from head to toe, or from their feet to the ends of their fingers and to their heads. Other people, after practice, only need to take a deep breath, stretch their arms and legs by extending them, tensing them, and then letting all the tension in their bodies go all at once. Whatever works best for you, it's important that you practice the relaxation exercises until you can reach a relaxed state on cue, whenever you desire it. In several of the techniques that are going to be explained now, you will use relaxation to reach a calm, comfortable state before you employ the technique.

BEHAVIOR REHEARSAL IN IMAGERY

The purpose of this technique is to try out in your imagination different ways of behaving in new or unfamiliar situations. This type of private rehearsal will help you feel more comfortable when you finally appear before a "live audience." The real experience, though new, will be familiar to you; it will seem natural, almost as if you had been there before. Through the imaginal practice you will also be programming yourself to feel confident and be successful in the new situation. It's similar to acting. Just as an actress rehearses a new part, imagines herself in the role, being the person, so can you fill the new role you create for yourself.

You can use behavior rehearsal for a situation like an upcoming job interview. In order to set the stage you first have to familiarize yourself with the details of a job interview procedure: how an interview would progress, how the interviewer and a successful applicant might act during the interview. It's essential, however, that you be prepared for the real interview (see page 282, "The Job Interview"). Then you are ready to create the scene and play the role in imagery.

Step One. Practice relaxation exercises in a quiet place where you can be sure you won't be disturbed. Then, when your body is fully relaxed and your mind is clear to create vivid and detailed images, you are ready to start.

Step Two. Picture yourself on the day of the interview. You stop to look at your reflection in a store window on your way to the interview. You approve of the way you are dressed and groomed. You like your look: womanly, with an executive snap. As you walk down the street your step is brisk, purposeful; your head is up, your body relaxed and comfortable. You are enthusiastic about the job opportunity and you feel a calm satisfaction within that you will present yourself favorably. You've allowed enough time in order to arrive a few minutes early. See yourself entering the building now, waiting calmly for the elevator. You enter the office and without hesitating approach the receptionist and give her your name. You hear your voice sounding clear and steady, the tone is cordial though businesslike. As you sit down to wait, you are feeling at ease. You casually observe your surroundings and other people entering or leaving the office. After a while you are called and you enter the interviewer's office. You move easily toward him as he gets up from his desk. You are standing straight but not rigid, looking directly at him. You feel your face relaxed, your arms comfortably at your sides, your weight balanced over both feet. You sit down, poised and relaxed. You appear self-assured and confident. . . .

Let the scene unfold in your imagination as you create the dialogue and your role the way you would like it to go. When you prepare yourself realistically for a positive experience in imagery, you increase the likelihood of a positive outcome.

You can also practice behavior rehearsal in real life. In this case, for instance, with a friend playing the role of interviewer.

A tape recorder can be useful in recording both the relaxation instructions and descriptions of the scenes and playing them back to yourself.

Use elements of past experiences in which you were successful, to increase your confidence. Remind yourself of them. Keep yourself aware of the good feeling of being in control, confident, on top of things. Use that sense of confidence in the new situation.

But what if even imagining going for an interview or just thinking about entering a new situation pushes your panic button? In that case your anxiety level will be so high that it will interfere with practicing behavior rehearsal in imagery. You'll need a more gradual approach, one that will help reduce the anxiety that has become connected to those situations. You'll need what we call *gradual painless exposure*.

GRADUAL PAINLESS EXPOSURE

Gradual painless exposure (GPE) works by retraining your nervous system and replacing your long built-up anxious or fearful response to a situation with a relaxed response. You learned the anxious response long ago and it has stuck with you even though today there is no longer any real danger connected to the situation. It's what we call "conditioned" anxiety. GPE is a way of "deconditioning" that kind of anxiety.

The principle underlying GPE is quite simple. You can see it when a caring parent calms a child who is frightened by a new and fearful situation. For example, little Lisa is thrilled as well as scared of the merry-go-round at the amusement park: the loud, clanging music, the animals whirling around. As Lisa and her mother walk toward the carousel, Lisa stops about fifty feet away, clamps her hands over her ears, and whimpers, "Don't let's go there. I'm afraid." Her mother bends down, hugs her, and says calmly, "That's okay. Let's just stand here awhile and watch."

While they're looking, Lisa's mother points out to her the man who is running the merry-go-round. They move several feet closer, as mom points out three children, giggling and laughing in a chariot drawn by two giant wood swans. Very slowly, without Lisa being aware of it, her mother continues to move closer to the carousel. All the while she speaks calmly to Lisa and keeps her interested in different amusing aspects of the merry-go-round. By the time the carousel slows to a stop, Lisa is about twenty feet from the platform, Now, between rides, mom suggests they look at the painted figures, maybe even sit in one of the chariots while it's not moving, just to see what it feels like.

So far, Lisa's initial fears seem to have been calmed. Her mother might next offer to ride with her on one of the stationary horses, or even on one of the moving animals. But if Lisa should begin to get anxious, her mother must go back to where Lisa felt comfortable, or return the next day to approach the carousel over again.

Lisa's fear was being overcome two ways. First by the calming and *counteracting* effect of her mother's presence and conversation. Second, by the fact that while her mother was talking calmly to her she was being introduced in gradual, progressive steps to the fearful situation.

These two elements, a competing or counteranxiety agent and graded exposure, provide the basis for *systematic desensitization,* the technique most widely used today by behavior therapists in the treatment of fears and phobias. Dr. Joseph Wolpe, the acknowledged father of behavior therapy, is responsible for its development. He found that if a person was exposed in a gradual and controlled way to small doses of whatever it was they feared—while at the same time they were kept relaxed—their fear would gradually diminish. This is what happened with Lisa and the merry-go-round. Lisa's mother could easily control how small or large a dose of fear Lisa was given by how slowly or rapidly they approached the merry-go-round. But how does a behavior therapist inject a small dose of, say, fear of asking for a raise, or fear of speaking in public? That's where imagery comes in.

Preparing a Hierarchy

By imagining what you're afraid of, a little bit at a time, the effect is almost the same as gradually exposing yourself to the real thing. And, if you are relaxed during the procedure, the fear will weaken and disappear altogether. When you use gradual painless exposure (GPE) in imagery, then, the first thing you must do is prepare a series of scenes, all having to do with the main theme of your fear. Write them down in the order of least fearful to most fearful. This is called a *hierarchy*. There may be anywhere from six to ten items on a hierarchy. It will help to give each item a rating, in other words, just how much anxiety your think you would experience if you were in the actual situation. For this purpose you can use an anxiety scale ranging from zero (feeling perfectly calm) to 100 (feeling as if you are about to panic). Try to make up items that will fit in the mid-range as well as the extreme ends of the scale. We refer to this scale as SUD scale, which stands for subjective units of disturbance.

For instance, if you've just finished a pleasant meal with some of your best friends, had a few glasses of wine, and feel real mellow, your SUD level would be at about zero. If you wake up one morning and find that you've overslept because the alarm didn't go off, and you have just forty minutes to dress and get to the office for an important meeting, your SUD level would probably be up somewhere in the 40 to 70 range. It's a purely subjective measure. Your 40 might be someone else's 20, and vice versa. Check yourself right now.

What's your SUD rating? Use that as a baseline against which to gauge higher anxiety-generating situations.

When you rate the imaginary scenes on a fear hierarchy for use with GPE, it will naturally be only an approximation. But if you're uncertain whether to rate a scene 30 or 50, it's better to give it the higher rating.

You construct a hierarchy from your own experiences, real or imagined. Here, for example, is a hierarchy on the theme of rejection that one woman wrote. The number before each item is her anxiety, or SUD, rating.

10 I call the hairdresser and his receptionist tells me he's only seeing regular customers so he can't see me.

20 I ask the operator to get an outside line and she says she's too busy now.

30 I go to a restaurant and the head waiter doesn't pay any attention to me or a woman friend.

50 I apply for membership in a club and I'm turned down.

55 I ask for a new office and I'm turned down; it's given to one of my peers.

60 I call on a buyer and I'm told he's too busy to see me.

65 A buyer calls up and cancels an order.

70 I approach an out-of-town buyer at a convention and I get a cold shoulder.

75 I ask for a raise or a promotion and I'm turned down.

85 My subordinate is chosen to be my boss.

100 I'm being fired.

After the hierarchy the second essential ingredient of GPE is deep muscle relaxation. Dr. Wolpe found that relaxation was one of the most effective agents to use against anxiety. After all, it's impossible to be both relaxed and anxious at the same time. This is why relaxation will be used to counteract any anxiety that may be aroused by any of the items on the hierarchy. It's essential, therefore, that you take the time to learn and to master the skill of relaxing. You may need a week or more of daily practice of deep muscle relaxation exercises before you are successful at inducing a relaxation response on cue.

PRACTICING GRADUAL PAINLESS EXPOSURE (GPE)

Once you have your hierarchy of stressful situations prepared, and you've learned to relax yourself down to a zero SUD level, you're ready to use GPE. It's a good idea to write each scene on a separate index card and then arrange them in order of SUD rating, with the lowest one on top. Now, get yourself seated comfortably in a quiet room where you know you won't be interrupted. Put the index cards with your hierarchy scenes on a table beside you. Settle back, let your eyes close, and allow your body to slip into that calm, relaxed state that you have become so familiar with through the relaxation exercises. When you feel you are at about a SUD level of zero, open your eyes and read to yourself the scene described on the first card. Now close your eyes and visualize the scene clearly and in detail. Try to get a sense of actually *being in the scene*.

Continue imagining it for about eight seconds, and notice by how much your anxiety level rises, if at all. Since this is the first scene on your hierarchy, it should only make you slightly uncomfortable. Your level of anxiety might go up 5, 10 or 15 points. (If, however, for some reason you've underestimated the potency of the scene when arranging your hierarchy, and as you imagine it now you find yourself getting *very* anxious, say 25 or more, then stop imagining the scene immediately. This means you'll have to go over your hierarchy and change the SUD ratings or the order of scenes. You may have to add one or two milder ones and start with those.)

Now erase the scene from your mind and go back to relaxing. Focus on the pleasant sensations of allowing your body to go perfectly limp and your mind to become passive, unconcerned with any thoughts. Picture that private, peaceful fantasy place where you can drift away to and feel perfectly calm again. Have several fantasy scenes so you can alternate them. When you're down to zero, repeat the first scene and notice if it bothers you less now than it did the first time. Again, after eight seconds, erase the scene and bring yourself back down to zero. As soon as a scene no longer arouses any anxiety, which could be after just one, or in some cases three or more repetitions, you are ready to move up the hierarchy to the next scene. In any case, you should never move up to the next scene while the previous one continues to evoke more than 5 SUD.

The object is to always keep yourself as close to zero as possible. This way, each time you expose yourself in imagery to the anxiety-charged scene, even though it may raise you 10 or at most, 15 points, you're able to weaken the impact with an added charge of relaxation. Think of your relaxation ability as a fully charged battery pack, strong enough to drive away the negative forces of anxiety. An encounter with an anxiety-producing scene may drain some of your energy, but in between scenes you're able to recharge, and eventually neutralize anxiety until it loses its power. That's why you never want to take on a scene that's so strong that it cannot be neutralized by relaxation after one or two exposures.

You can practice GPE several times a week, or, at most, once a day. Limit your sessions to about thirty minutes. Progress through a hierarchy should not be rushed. You may go through two or three items successfully in just one session, or you may need to spend an entire session or two on one scene. When you feel perfectly at ease with a scene in imagery, then you're ready to experience it in real life. You'll be pleased to find that in the actual situation you are no longer bothered by the old feelings of tension and anxiety that used to be associated with it.

GPE takes time and patience, but I assure you, the rewards are worth it. Remember, take your time. One step at a time. Gradually, slowly, you can train yourself to react in new ways to old cues.

Not only do the images you create of situations, yourself, and others influence your attitudes and feelings, but so too do the thoughts and statements you silently make to yourself about them. The following technique shows you how self-talk can be utilized to enhance your own self-image and to alter your attitudes toward events or situations that might otherwise upset you.

SELF-STATEMENTS—EVALUATING SELF-TALK

Most of us get into the habit of making negative self-statements, because critical remarks are so prevalent in our surroundings. Approving of oneself and acknowledging and enjoying one's competencies and assets are often frowned upon. Most religious teachings stress the virtue of modesty. Schoolchildren are often criticized by their peers for being "stuck-up" or "full of yourself," or having a "swelled head." These are all comments about thinking positively about oneself! To think highly of oneself often incurs the censure of others. Therefore we grow up with the idea that liking or approving of oneself is wrong.

How often have you heard parents criticize or find fault with their children?

"You're all thumbs, just like your father. Can't you ever do anything right?"

"You don't get your shyness from *my* side of the family."

"Look at those grades! An Einstein you'll never be!"

"She'll never be the student Ellie was—but at least she's pretty."

"You think of nobody but yourself. I've never known anyone so selfish!"

The sad truth is that while we are growing up, most of us hear more negative than positive things said to us and about us by parents, siblings, and peers. Many of these derogatory remarks and appraisals stick with us and we accept them as valid. As we grow older, we adopt this negative mode of thinking for our own, and the habit of making negative self-statements becomes established. Some women are more fortunate to have been raised in a home where attention was given to the positive aspects of their personalities. Chances are that these women will develop healthier, more positive views of themselves, because they will continue making these statements to themselves subvocally.

Unfortunately this is not true for most of us. We grow up accepting negative beliefs about ourselves and go on to turn them into negative self-statements. This permeates our attitudes, our way of thinking, what we say to ourselves about our abilities and our desirableness and our status in life. Eventually it becomes a habitual way of viewing ourselves and the world.

But we can change this by consciously altering those self-statements. By being aware of the positive things we do and making complimentary statements to ourselves about them, we can change our attitude and behavior.

You're probably thinking that is more easily said than done. True, you won't do it overnight, but little by little, step-by-step, every day will bring you that much closer to your goal. With a little daily conscious effort you can replace old attitudes and views with new and positive ones.

Take Mary Ellen, for instance. Every time she completed a

report and handed it to her boss, she would walk away from his office reprimanding herself for not having done a better job, and reviewing in her mind all the things she was certain he'd find fault with. She always ended up feeling dissatisfied and with a low opinion of herself. This, despite the fact that in the two and a half years she had been working for him, her boss's comments to her about her work had always been positive ones.

Once she became aware of the negative, self-defeating statements she had been making to herself, she practiced consciously changing them to positive ones. After handing in a report, she now said to herself, "Well, I really did a thorough job on that report!" or "I pinpointed a lot of important issues in that analysis. I know it will prove productive," and mentally patted herself on the back.

When you start becoming more aware of your positives and less focused on negatives, you strengthen your personal support system and enhance your self-image.

Every time you do something you like, no matter how small it is, make a positive statement to yourself: "I handled that well," or "I like the way I took care of that problem." Even in situations that are not overall successes, pick out *something* positive you did and dwell on that.

Successful women's histories often show that they were encouraged to be action-oriented. Your self-talk may be geared to keeping you passive as opposed to taking action. Positive self-statements are one way of changing a view of yourself as a passive person to a more action-oriented one. For example, tell yourself, "I am competent. Let's see what I can do to change the situation." When you find yourself saying something that seems like a put-down, "I can't do this," or "This requires more education than I have," deliberately change the negative statements to positive ones.

Because we're continuously talking to ourselves subvocally, and responding to what we say *autonomically*, we have a great deal of latitude for changing our responses. We accept what we say as truth, and then we respond to it. In turn, our environment responds to the way we respond to that statement. A vicious cycle can be set up.

The first step is to become aware of what you're saying to yourself. In a given situation you may only be aware of the *feeling* of discomfort or anxiety. With practice you'll be able to connect that feeling to some statement you were making to yourself about the situation or yourself. A good way to do this is to carry with you several index cards or a pocket-size memo pad. Every day, whenever you are aware of a negative or self-defeating thought, write it down on a separate card or page. The thoughts may be more prevalent than you think and, like a picture flashed briefly on a screen, difficult to grasp. If you're feeling down or discouraged, uptight or frightened, ask yourself, "What am I saying to myself right now about this situation or about myself?" At the end of the day read over your list of negative thoughts. Then see how many are exaggerated, irrational, or unrealistic. Ask yourself, "What evidence do I have to support that negative statement?" In the space below change each thought to a realistic and positive one. You'll be surprised at the number of unproductive things you say to yourself in the course of a workday.

Suppose, for example, you're feeling a little apprehensive about going to a cocktail party given by your boss. You become aware of the following thoughts: "They won't be interested in what I have to say; I won't be able to join in on their conversations. I'll sound like a real dummy." Then you deliberately change those statements to more realistic, positive ones: "I'm as knowledgeable as the average person in many areas, and I'm more knowledgeable in some. And if the topic is over my head, I can be a good listener. I'm not going there to be tested or judged; I'm going to socialize."

Claudia was one of the few women executives in her department who hadn't finished college. After a week of monitoring her self-talk, she became aware of how often she was saying, "I don't have a college degree. I don't have the formal education everyone else here has." She was able to trace her feelings of discomfort and inferiority around her colleagues directly to those and similar negative self-statements. She practiced replacing them with realistic and constructive statements, such as: "I have a lot of smarts. My skills are my own special smarts. I'm perceptive and creative, that's why I'm in this job. I have a quick mind, and that's not something that's given out with college diplomas."

I want to emphasize the importance of writing down your thoughts and disputing them on paper. It puts you in a better position to evaluate them objectively; to see clearly the faulty reasoning the way you might if a friend had made the same statements.

The following is another method designed to help you build a more positive self-image. It's especially helpful if you've been carrying around a lot of negatively biased views of yourself. Try to be as objective and unprejudiced toward yourself as you can when you do this exercise.

APPRECIATING YOURSELF

I'm sure at some time in your life you've heard the familiar complaint: "He [or she] takes me for granted. He doesn't appreciate all the things I do for him."

Did it ever occur to you that you might be taking yourself for granted? Not giving credit where credit's due? I'd like you to reintroduce yourself to you. Become reacquainted with yourself, with the many facets of your personality, the positive qualities, all the assets you possess but may have been taking for granted or ignoring. You may have abilities you downgrade because they're yours—abilities you might admire in someone else.

This is a healthy exercise in self-appreciation. You are going to take an inventory of all your assets—talents, skills, competencies, accomplishments—past and present. Review your life experiences and see how many were learning experiences. Today there are a number of universities that recognize that important learning takes place outside as well as inside the classroom. For adults reentering graduate or undergraduate programs, they will assess and award credits on the basis of life experience.

So get a pencil and paper and begin your inventory. Think of the projects, hobbies, activities you were involved in at school, after school; summer jobs, part-time jobs. Think of the crises you've dealt with, the problems in living you've resolved, and how you've learned and grown as a result of them. Get the sum total of you. List both the things you have learned and done well and those you consider important. Big and small things you've accomplished. Don't discount small achievements; they are often the groundwork that later strengths are built upon. Rummage through your past and explore all areas where you have capabilities. What are they?

Vivian was forty-one, divorced, and with two grown children who, for the first time this year, would both be living away from home. She was bored with the executive secretarial job she had held for six years. She felt stuck, and with her feelings of self-worth at an all-time low, was experiencing a serious identity crisis. Although she was eligible for her company's executive training program, she just couldn't see herself in the role of an executive. She didn't believe she had the potential, or "what it takes" to be an executive. Then she set aside an evening to review and reassimilate her past experiences. Here is her list:

- At thirteen, largest number of merit badges in scout troop; elected leader of my troop.

- Counselor at summer camp. Developed patience and understanding of children; learned how to handle lots of conflict situations.
- Reporter on high school paper; got over shyness interviewing people in all walks of life.
- Assistant editor of yearbook.
- Summer work at father's office. Learned basics of accounting; learned to take charge when he was away.
- Made all arrangements for sister's wedding; learned how to handle some sticky situations.
- Two summer writers' workshops. Published two short stories that year.
- Raised two children currently pursuing careers, one in law, one in business.
- Stuck to my decision to get out of a destructive marriage, despite family opposition. (I've learned to make my own decisions and take full responsibility for the consequences.)
- Kept my cool following son's auto accident. Handled claim on my own efficiently.
- Dealt diplomatically with principal following Susie's near-expulsion from high school.
- Recruited volunteers for political campaign; learned to raise funds.
- Organized parents' group to support salary raise for teachers.
- Streamlined present job when I took over. Eliminated trivia so that office functioned more effectively than before.
- Introduced innovative ideas in office procedure.

Vivian's inventory-taking expanded her view of herself, reminded her of her competencies, and boosted her self-esteem. She got a more realistic image of herself and realized that much of her experience—acting effectively in emergencies, making decisions and sticking to them, handling people, organizing projects—actually equipped her quite well to handle the responsibilities and organizational demands of an executive position. She joined the training program where her executive potential was quickly recognized. She's now well on her way up in management.

Sometimes, hard as you may try to create positive images or thoughts about yourself or your performance, you can't seem to dislodge certain persistent, negative thoughts from your mind. You recognize the irrationality of these self-defeating thoughts but they refuse to go away. The next technique provides you with a powerful mind-controling tool for eliminating such intrusive thoughts.

THOUGHT-STOPPING

If positive self-statements don't work as well as you want them to, try this technique.

Whether we are aware of it or not, you and I and everyone are continually talking to ourselves. There is a constant stream of subvocalization going on. The process works much like this: We make a statement about something to ourselves, and respond emotionally to the statement we make. We don't realize that we can change the thought or the statement, and thus change the way we feel about a situation.

For instance, Mary had to give a report at a sales meeting. She had been preoccupied for several days before the meeting about the performance. Some of her negative thoughts were, "What if my voice cracks?" "What if my boss sees my hand shaking? He'll think I'm unqualified for the responsible position I'm holding." As a result, she became more anxious as the day approached.

I showed her how to employ thought-stopping in this man-

ner: I asked her to close her eyes, deliberately think the anxiety-provoking thought, and to signal me when the thought
was clear in her mind. Then I slammed a book down on the
table, at the same time shouting *"Stop!"* Mary was startled,
and looked at me in confusion. I asked her what happened to
the thought. "It disappeared," she said.

I asked her to do it again; this time instead of shouting the
word *"Stop!"* I instructed her to shout *"Stop!"* herself. She
did this. Finally I had her, instead of shouting *"Stop!"* say it
subvocally, or to see the word in her mind's eye. When she was
able to do this successfully I suggested she switch her thinking
to a pleasant thought, such as a beautiful beach or a relaxing
scene in the woods or a party where she had been happy.

In your first attempts to use thought-stopping you may find
the old thoughts sometimes recur. Don't be discouraged. The
effectiveness of thought-stopping depends on the frequency
with which you practice it. Persistence and repetition are
important. Teach yourself thought-stopping and use it when
you find yourself bothered by a negative or intrusive
thought.

When a thought keeps coming into your mind, you may
begin to ruminate on it. For example, Anne Marie had a bad
failure—she got fired from her last job, even though it wasn't
her fault. She kept thinking it would happen again, and worried about it. Every time her boss got angry, she thought,
"Oh, I'm going to get fired again."

What should she do? First, pick out a positive coping statement. "I'm doing a competent job. I really know what I'm
doing. He has a problem. His problem has nothing to do with
my competence." Then, whenever she found herself thinking,
"I'm going to get fired," she stopped the thought by shouting
to herself, *"Stop!"* and then switched to one of the positive
coping statements she had prepared.

At conferences Harriet frequently found herself holding
back from offering suggestions or ideas. It wasn't that she

didn't have any, but she made herself uptight and fearful of contributing, with persistent negative thoughts such as, "If I open my mouth, I'll put my foot in it." "If I say something, it'll be the wrong thing." "Once I start talking they'll find out I'm a phoney." Harriet was creative and capable, but her confidence was being undermined by these recurring self-destructive thoughts that she seemed unable to control.

She first prepared herself with the following positive statements all based on reality: "My ideas come from my experience, and they're as valid as anyone else's." "I didn't get this far by fooling people; I made it through the quality of my work." "The purpose of this meeting is to exchange ideas and offer suggestions; it's not a contest." Then she began practicing thought-stopping at her next conference, and before the conference ended she was feeling more at ease and comfortable enough to make several significant contributions. It wasn't long before Harriet's view of herself changed to a more realistic and positive one, and her self-assurance increased.

Next is one of my own personal approaches to contending with worrisome thoughts.

MAKING AN APPOINTMENT WITH YOURSELF

This is like thought-stopping. When it's inappropriate or inconvenient to think about something, make an appointment with yourself to think about it later. Write on a calendar or in your date book: "Think about the new job," or "Decide what to do about Mr. Z. at work." This technique helps you handle obsessive thoughts. For example, if you wake up in the middle of the night with ideas about what to do in a situation, and you can't go back to sleep, make an appointment with yourself to handle it in the morning. "At 10:00 A.M. I'll sit down and go over this with a piece of paper. Then I'll handle it." This technique helps you to budget your time more efficiently, and to control what you're thinking about and when.

Just as no amount of reading or imagery training will enable you to swim or ski if you've never done it before, learning any new behavior requires doing it. When you are ready, that is to say, feeling relatively nonanxious, start with the easy steps first and then move up. Learning new behavior calls for a gradual shaping procedure in real-life situations.

SHAPING NEW BEHAVIORS

This technique, like GPE, requires building a hierarchy, but unlike GPE the situations are not associated with anxiety. They are graded tasks, ranging in degree of difficulty, and related to a new behavior or habit you'd like to acquire. The purpose is to learn a new skill or behavior through a gradual shaping process.

Chris was not particularly active socially. She had a couple of close friends she saw on weekends, but had enough interests to keep herself busy so that it didn't bother her when she didn't see them. She realized that if she was to move up in her field, she'd have to get out more and extend her circle of friends and acquaintances. Chris was personable and comfortable with people. She simply had never given much importance to socializing. She planned a training program for herself to develop new social habits. Here is her hierarchy:

- At the end of the day, spend more time talking to people before leaving the office.
- Get into a conversation during coffee break with someone I'd like to know better.
- Ask someone I know out to lunch (Karen or Diane).
- Ask someone new out to lunch (Priscilla or Betty).

- Suggest a theater date with three friends at work.
- Suggest a dinner date with two or three other friends at work.
- Join a women's club or health club that I know other business associates belong to.
- Have two or three friends to my apartment for drinks Saturday afternoon.
- Have one or two friends for dinner at my apartment.
- Give a party for seven or eight people at my home.

When you practice an unfamiliar behavior by planned, progressive steps, you'll be able to develop new, productive habits without too much effort. You can train yourself in the same way to develop a new skill. If, however, you find yourself avoiding many of the situations you planned because they arouse anxiety, then you'll need to start with behavior rehearsal in imagery or GPE.

One of the best aids to developing a new skill or behavioral style is a model, that is, someone you can learn from by observing; someone who is effective and has a style you admire.

MODELING

According to social learning psychologists most of what we learn as children is through imitation of others, such as parents, older siblings, or peers. They call it *modeling*. Even as adults we continue to learn, unconsciously, by modeling styles or behaviors of people we admire.

But we can also use modeling consciously as a learning tool on the job, in our profession, or socially. Let's say, for instance, that one of your problems is organization. You just can't seem to keep your desk looking neat, to find the notes or papers you need when you want them, to keep your files in order, or to line up your appointments without bumping into yourself. Look around and notice who appears to be well organized. Who gets the most done with the least amount of effort? Then observe her closely for a week and try doing some things the way she does them. If you're friendly with her, you might ask her for some tips.

If certain behaviors, such as giving orders or asserting yourself with superiors, give you trouble, watch someone who handles herself effectively, the way you would like to in those types of situations, and then try adopting some of her strategies. Now don't get the wrong idea. I'm not suggesting you mimic or impersonate someone else. Your goal is not to become a carbon copy of another person. Your goal is to observe how someone with qualities you admire behaves in certain situations and then to adapt those behaviors to your own style. You're not out to fake a skill you don't have or pretend to be something or someone you're not. Modeling will help you improve your performance and broaden your view of yourself. You can learn and incorporate elements of someone else's manner or style into your own unique style.

When you choose a model, make it someone you can realistically emulate. Choose someone who is in some ways like you, someone you would feel comfortable following. Research has shown that it is easier for us to learn from *coping* models, that is, from people who are more like ourselves, who are fallible and not perfect, than from models of perfection.

The next is another imagery technique, one that trains you to react with less fear to particular people you may have difficulty dealing with, either because of their position of authority, their intimidating manner, or both. It's a harmless way of transforming them into ordinary, vulnerable human beings, just like the rest of us. It is, in effect, a humanizing process.

Humanizing a Person

With this technique you imagine a person who makes you anxious, and put them in a nonthreatening or amusing situation. Imagine the boss walking his baby at night. Humanize him. A change in your perceptions will make you behave differently around him.

We all have fantasies we build up about what people are and we respond to these fantasies. When we change the fantasies, that is, change what we are responding to, then *how* we respond will change. If you feel anxious or uptight around someone, like a supervisor or boss, you may be giving that person more power in your own mind than he or she really has. When you think of the person in absurd or ordinary at-home situations he or she will be less threatening. Imagine a gruff boss dressed in a baseball uniform or in a frogman suit. Picture the intimidating supervisor alone at home in the evening, wearing pajamas with a Donald Duck design, asleep in front of his TV set, snoring loudly.

There may actually be more of reality in the humanizing image you create of the person than in the fear-inspiring image you are carrying around with you. Try humanizing some of those authority figures you usually feel uncomfortable with and see how much more natural you will feel around them.

The strategies that are described next can help you to directly manage or shape the behavior of others.

TIME-OUT AND REINFORCEMENT PROCEDURES

These are two basic tactics of behavior modifiers: Reinforce the behavior to be increased; ignore the behavior to be decreased. Praise an employee for a job well done. Reward the employee who puts out extra effort to help you on a deadline. You'll be increasing the chances that he'll help you again in the future. At work we all need positive feedback—other than a paycheck—to let us know we're doing a good job or that our extra efforts are appreciated. Words of praise or appreciation mean a lot. As a manager be generous—and judicious—in giving them. When a supervisor habitually reels off a string of "Terrific!" "Great!" "Good job!" indiscriminately and regardless of the quality of the work, the reinforcing effect soon wears thin.

On the other hand, when you give someone "time-out" you deliberately ignore them while they are behaving in a particularly annoying or offensive way. The purpose is to discourage them from continuing. Knowledgeable parents do it with their children. They'll ignore the temper tantrum and eventually the child learns it doesn't work. When the child finds a more appropriate way to express himself or herself, the parents will be quick to reinforce the child for it. A mother's advice to her teary-eyed little girl carries the same message: "The next time Bobby talks to you that way, just ignore him and walk away. He's only doing it to get a rise out of you."

When Mr. Smith slips a seductive remark or off-color joke into his conversation with Beverly, she turns away and occupies herself with some papers on her desk. Then, as soon as he gets back on track, she gives him her undivided attention. If Beverly is consistent in giving him time-out whenever he gets into personal or sexual topics, it won't be long before he gets the message and the behavior that annoys Beverly gets extinguished.

Give time-out to a talkative colleague by selectively ignoring her when she gossips. But don't forget the flip side: Reinforce her by showing interest and giving her your attention when she has more constructive things to say.

These are important principles of behavioral shaping that

you will want to keep in mind when dealing with subordinates or bosses on the job.

ASSERTIVENESS

This technique, or, more accurately, group of techniques, is so important that I am going to devote all of the following chapter to it.

5 ASSERTIVENESS

Susan is a junior executive in a large corporation. One morning her boss calls her in and introduces her to an out-of-town executive of the company.

BOSS: Susan, this is Fred Smith. He's in town for a week, and I told him he could use your office while he's here. Hope you don't mind. . . . You can share space with Helen for the time being. Fred's brought a lot of work with him, and I don't mean to rush you, but it would be a big help if he could set up right away.

SUSAN (smiling nervously, looking down at her folded hands): Oh, that's fine with me . . . no problem. I'll move my stuff out right away.

BOSS: Good for you. I knew you'd help us out.

SMITH: Hey, I hate to do this to you, Susan. You sure you don't mind?

SUSAN: Oh, of course not. It's perfectly okay. I don't mind at all.

But the truth, as you may have guessed, is that Susan *does* mind, and it's *not* perfectly okay with her. Back in her office, as she empties her desk, she feels hurt, put down and taken advantage of. In spite of her seniority and executive position, she suddenly feels very unimportant. "That's just great," she thinks angrily. "Nobody cares how *I* feel about things. I obviously don't matter much around here." Her hurt changes to anger, and then deep, smoldering resentment.

Then why is Susan so compliant? Why doesn't she say how she really feels? Why is she so anxious to please? Susan is *nonassertive*. She doesn't know how to stand up for her rights.

Let's look at how someone else might handle the same situation. Andrea knows how to assert herself appropriately. This is how she would behave if her boss made the same announcement to her.

ANDREA (looking directly at him): That's going to be a real inconvenience for me, Mr. Gruman. It'll interrupt my work schedule and make it awkward for customers who have appointments with me this week. Frankly, I'm quite upset. Don't you think we can make some other arrangement for Fred, instead of evicting me from my office?

BOSS: I'm sorry, Andrea. Your office was the first one I thought of. I had such short notice . . . and I really didn't think you'd mind. I already told Fred he could use your office this morning. Guess I should have asked you first.

ANDREA: Yes, that would have been better. Look, Mr. Gruman, I know it's a sticky situation and I'd be willing to let him use my office today, since I'll be out most of the day anyway. But I'm not willing to give it up for the entire week.

BOSS: All right, Andrea, let me see if I can work out something else. Sorry, I didn't realize it was so important to you.

ANDREA: Thanks, Mr. Gruman. I'll appreciate that.

Andrea, unlike Susan, is *assertive*. She's able to stand up for her rights. She knows how to express herself firmly and appropriately. But suppose the boss had made his announcement to Jackie, another woman who, like Susan, needs to learn assertive skills. The trouble with Jackie is that she goes to the other extreme. She overreacts and shows a lot of misdirected hostility. She has learned that she can often get her way by being overbearing and pushy. Jackie isn't assertive; she's *aggressive*. After getting such an announcement from her boss, Jackie plants her hands on her hips and gives him a chilly stare.

JACKIE: Great! Who elected me? I just love the way everybody pushes me around to suit their own convenience. You could at least have had some consideration for my feelings. Is Fred more important than I am? There are other offices here besides mine. . . . You men really stick together, don't you. I suppose you all just assume we're ready and willing to move over whenever you want. Well I'll be damned if I'll move out of my office! The least you could do is—"

BOSS: Just a minute, Jackie, now just slow down. Take it easy. This is a touchy situation, let's not make it any worse than it is. We can do without the dramatics, too, by the way. Go back to your office and calm down. I'll make some other arrangements.

Jackie turns, storms out of the office, and slams the door behind her.

You've just seen how three different women handled the same situation. The first was nonassertive. The second appropriately assertive. And the third overly aggressive. Let's look more closely at the differences in their behavior.

SUSAN—NONASSERTIVE

1. Doesn't express her honest feelings
2. Doesn't clearly state her needs or wishes
3. Ignores her own rights
4. Is anxious to please and avoid conflict
5. Avoids eye contact
6. Shows poor, submissive, body posture

Susan's nonassertive behavior leaves her feeling angry, frustrated and resentful. What's worse, she feels inadequate. She feels ineffectual, unimportant. She dislikes herself, and puts herself down for not standing up for herself. Her self-esteem is lowered, and she goes on wondering why she doesn't get the same respect from her boss that he gives to other executives. Meanwhile, she's gotten a reputation for being a "good guy," someone who can always be counted on, and sometimes taken advantage of. She'll probably continue to give in to the needs of others and resent it, because she must at all cost avoid conflict. And the cost may be high. Held-in anger and built-up resentment strain relationships outside the office as well as inside. It's a good way to develop ulcers and high blood pressure. Susan's negative feelings about herself may lower her self-esteem so far that she gets seriously depressed.

A woman who has trouble being assertive with her boss or co-workers may find it easy to assert herself with her boyfriend or husband or children. But then they may be the ones who get the brunt of her pent-up anger from the office. If any of these situations seem to apply to you, you may need to brush up your assertive skills. Lack of assertiveness takes its greatest toll in the damage it does to your self-respect. You may be fooling yourself about your nonassertiveness by telling yourself that you are just being polite, or that you don't like to hurt other people's feelings, or that you're easygoing, or something's just not worth getting upset over. You may find it much easier to say yes and avoid the discomfort and guilt you might feel if you said no. But you may find that you feel annoyed with yourself because you didn't say something when you had the chance to. Or you feel put down or taken advantage of. If this is true of you, you may, like Susan, be acting in a nonassertive way.

ANDREA—ASSERTIVE
1. Expresses her feelings appropriately
2. States her needs
3. Suggests alternative solutions
4. Offers compromise, saying clearly what she is willing and not willing to do
5. Shows respect for the needs of others
6. Makes eye contact

Everyone benefits from appropriate assertive behavior. It makes for clear communication. It leaves no uncertainty about people's needs and expectations of one another. It fosters mutual respect and cooperation.

Andrea doesn't hide the fact that she's upset. She communicates how she feels about her boss's decision using "I" language. She doesn't attack him personally or argue about his decision. She expresses her understanding of his needs, and makes a clear statement of hers, and of her expectations. As a result she feels good about herself. She feels effective and satisfied with how she handled the situation. Her boss, too, because she was respectful and honest with him, will want to make an effort to accommodate her. He is aware of her needs only because she has told him what they are.

Too often unassertive people make the mistake of hoping or expecting that others will know what they want. Then they are disappointed when people fail to have ESP, and they end up hurt and resentful. For example, an unassertive woman might think: "If Frances was a good friend she'd have brought me back a cup of coffee from the cafeteria. I really resent her being so thoughtless." What she means is: "If Frances was a good friend she would have read my mind, known what I wanted, not make it necessary for me to assert myself and ask her to do something for me, and brought me back a coffee from upstairs."

JACKIE—AGGRESSIVE

It's a common mistake to confuse assertiveness with aggressiveness. In some ways they appear similar. Aggressive and assertive people are both expressive, and often both get what they want. Jackie

1. Expresses her feelings inappropriately, with sarcasm and anger
2. Shouts her demands
3. Allows no room for compromise
4. Fails to show respect for others
5. Has a belligerent way of standing or sitting
6. Depreciates the boss and puts him on the defensive
7. Dominates the conversation

Jackie may feel better for having "expressed herself," but emotional outbursts and slamming doors communicate nothing of value. They don't help build better relationships. Jackie's boss will think of her as touchy, hysterical, and insulting. He may respond by a counterattack, and be just as aggressive. Or he may give in to her on this issue, chalk it up as a nuisance, and place her name on the list of employees soon to be let go. Jackie isn't aware that aggression causes others to become hostile, puts them down, makes them feel defensive, and want to retaliate. The aggressive woman who plays tough is often avoided. Her colleagues may not think much of her and her subordinates may fear and dislike her.

Ellen was an energetic, ambitious buyer for a large retail chain. She was so aggressive she bruised many people's egos. At thirty-four she was rapidly rising in her company, with a reputation for being a tough and aggressive go-getter. Unfortunately, she made enemies of the people whose toes she had stepped on. Her future at the company looked good to her. But a year later, when her department was reorganized, Ellen was shocked to find that instead of a promotion she was offered a post as assistant buyer in one of their branches.

Ellen failed to realize how important it is to build good relationships. She wasn't aware of the feelings of others or respectful of them. She intimidated her subordinates and made her colleagues resent her.

If you are genuinely assertive you show your strength by communicating your ideas and instructions clearly, by being open, and by respecting the needs and rights of others. In a recently published interview, a top woman executive in the film industry was quoted as saying she would like to think of herself as a strong woman, not a tough woman. The difference between the two is what separates assertiveness from aggression.

Dr. Joseph Wolpe, professor of psychiatry at Temple University, was one of the first to recognize the importance of assertiveness training in the practice of behavior therapy. He describes assertive behavior as "the proper expression of any emotion, other than anxiety toward another person."

How do *you* rate on assertiveness? Test yourself now by seeing how easy or difficult it would be for you to handle the following situations. Score yourself on this scale, from one to five:

1. *Very easy* (I'd feel perfectly comfortable)
2. *Easy* (I might feel slightly uncomfortable)

3. *Not so easy* (I would be uncomfortable)
4. *Very difficult* (I'd be very uncomfortable)
5. *Extremely difficult* (I'm not sure I could do it)

RATING

1. Ask for something from my boss, such as time off. ( )
2. Cut short a phone conversation with a very
   talkative co-worker. ( )
3. Tell a subordinate I'm not satisfied with his or
   her work. ( )
4. Ask a secretary to retype a letter a third time. ( )
5. Ask a supervisor to repeat his or her instructions
   for a job I'm doing. ( )
6. Ask for a raise. ( )
7. Turn down somebody who's soliciting money for
   a charity. ( )
8. Say no when I'm asked to work late. ( )
9. Ask someone who's using the copying machine to
   let me run off my copies before he or she finishes
   a much longer job. ( )
10. Accept criticism of my work from my supervisor,
    and ask for his or her ideas about how I can
    improve. ( )
11. Tell a co-worker he or she's done something to
    offend me. ( )
12. Delegate authority. ( )
13. Say "I don't know" when I'm asked about some-
    thing I truly don't have an answer for. ( )
14. Turn down a transfer that's offered to me
    because it doesn't fit my career plans. ( )
15. Stick to a decision I believe in, even though others
    oppose it. ( )

16. Excuse myself early or in the middle of an office meeting. ( )
17. Be the one to bring the discussion back on target when someone goes off on a tangent during a conference. ( )
18. Turn down a co-worker who asks me for a date. ( )
19. Accept a compliment from my boss graciously. ( )
20. Give a compliment to a subordinate. ( )
21. Quit my job when it becomes clear that I can't move up any higher in the company. ( )
22. Tell a man at work that I don't like being called "honey" or "sweetie." ( )
23. Give my opinions when I know other people will disagree with me. ( )

Now add up your score and see which category you fit into.

20 to 50 Assertive
50 to 75 Moderately assertive
75 to 90 Unassertive
90 to 110 Very unassertive

This quiz gives only a very general picture of your assertive ability. Sometimes circumstances make it easier to be assertive, and sometimes more difficult. It may be easier for you to talk to a subordinate about her inferior work when she is younger than you and the setting is casual and informal. It may be harder to do if she's an older woman. And it may be very difficult if the subordinate is an older man. If you rate yourself very low on assertiveness you might find it helpful to join a workshop in assertiveness training.

There are also many good books on assertion. *Your Perfect Right* by Robert Alberti and Michael L. Emmons, and *When I Say No, I Feel Guilty* by Manuel Smith, are two you will find extremely useful.

NONVERBAL ASSERTIVENESS

Body Language

Even before you start to talk, you are telling people a lot about yourself by the way you stand and walk, and by the expression on your face. The silent language of your body is very important to the way people respond to you. Here are some of the ways your body speaks. Start noticing them in yourself and others.

Posture. Do you sit stiffly on the edge of your chair? Slouch when you're standing? Maybe you shift your weight from one foot to another or fidget with your hands behind your back when you talk to a boss or prospective client. If you do, your body language is not likely to inspire confidence. It's most likely to tell people you're insecure, unsure of yourself. When you shift from one foot to the other it communicates to them you are easily manipulated.

If you think this applies to you, try to create an image of yourself talking to your boss in an assertive, confident way. See yourself standing erect but not rigid, your weight evenly balanced on both legs, so your feet are firmly on the floor. Your arms are relaxed by your sides, or perhaps both hands are clasped loosely in front of you. Your head is up, you are looking directly at the boss.

Eye contact. Good eye contact is probably the most essential part of assertive communication. Good eye contact says, "I'm interested in what you are saying. I hear you." Or, "I'm sincere about what I'm saying. It's important to me that you hear me." In conversation, look into the face of the person you're communicating with. Don't allow your eyes to wander around the room. Keep them fixed on the other person. You can shift your focus from eyes to nose to forehead to chin, and so on, while still appearing to maintain eye contact. Good eye contact is a very easy skill to practice. Think how you respond to someone who speaks to you with shifty eyes. They probably seem insecure or even not honest, as they avoid looking at you, shift around nervously, and stare at the wall behind you or at the floor. You may feel uneasy with them and wonder whether they are interested in what you're saying.

Make a point of practicing good eye contact. At first it may seem awkward, but you will soon feel comfortable with it. It can help to try it with friends.

Facial expression and gestures. Your gestures and facial expression need to harmonize with the verbal message you're giving. If they don't, your verbal message is weakened and you may not be believed. If you are angry at a shipping clerk and complaining to him about repeated errors, it won't do to wear an apologetic grin while you tell him he has to do better. Or perhaps you can remember seeing someone give a presentation of an exciting idea but doing it with such a deadpan face that the idea didn't seem exciting at all. Chances are that words alone will not be enough to convey excitement and enthusiasm to listeners. If you think of the exciting people you've listened to, you'll become aware of how much of their enthusiasm is communicated through their faces and gestures. You may find it useful to try this experiment. Look at yourself in the mirror. Now knit your brows into a deep, furrowed frown, while you bring the corners of your mouth down in an angry sneer, and say with conviction: "This is the happiest day of my life."

Body language and facial expression should be compatible with verbal language or the clash weakens and strains the credibility of your message. Appropriate hand gestures and an earnest facial expression will emphasize the points you make, and keep your listeners interested. One of the best ways to improve your nonverbal communication is to practice in front of a mirror, or with a friend. Try the Silent Movie exercise: Practice a conversation without words. Use your body language, gestures, and facial expressions to show your thoughts and feelings.

VERBAL COMMUNICATION

Voice. Effective, versatile inflection adds impact to your conversation. If you speak in a soft, whispery voice you'll lose your audience. If you have a squeaky voice people will find it hard to take you seriously. So if you think you could use some exercises to improve your voice, see page 279, "Your Voice."

Content. The best rule to follow here is: Think before you speak. Ask yourself: What will be the consequences of what I'm saying, on the other person and on myself? What will be the long-term effects? Am I considering my needs as well as those of the other person? It is important to have balance and mutual respect. The Talmud says, "If I am not for myself, who will be for me? But if I am for myself alone, what am I?"

Timing. Choose the appropriate time and place. It's unwise to criticize someone while he or she is with a group of other employees. Reprimands or grievances should be discussed in private. If you decide to approach your boss for a raise, pick the time and place where he or she will be most open to your request.

Assertive skills will make it possible for you to communicate clearly with others. The following four pointers are helpful.

1. *Make a direct, honest statement of your thoughts, your position, or your intentions.* It is important to let people know where you stand and what you're willing and not willing to do. You need to set limits for others, which make clear just what

is expected of you and what you expect of them. If you ask a vague question, you will probably get an unclear answer, and someone may end up disappointed and angry. If you begin a project "assuming" what is needed or expected, you could wander far off course before you realize you're making a mistake. Take time to ask specific questions and get specific answers.

Some people have the habit of asking questions that are really hidden requests. This is not good assertive behavior. For example, Mary's boss tells her he has scheduled a meeting for 4:00 P.M. Mary is dismayed by the late hour. "Do you really want to schedule the meeting so late in the day?" Mary asks. What she means is: "I don't think it's such a great idea." But her question is manipulative and vague. If her boss isn't a mind reader, he'll just say "Yes," and that will be the end of it.

Mary could say, assertively: "I noticed you've scheduled the meeting for four o'clock. I'd prefer it if you set an earlier hour—say, one or two. Would you agree to a change?" Here Mary honestly expresses her feelings, and makes a direct request.

Or take the example of Karen, whose boss approaches her at three-thirty on Friday:

"You don't mind working a little late tonight, do you, Karen?" he asks.

"Oh, no. Of course not," Karen responds. What she means is, "Shoot! There go my dinner plans!" Karen isn't being honest. She'll end up doing something she doesn't want to do, and resent the boss for it. She'll also hate herself for being weak-willed. Karen could have answered, assertively: "I'm sorry, I can't tonight. But if you want I'll make plans to stay late on Monday." By saying that, Karen is being honest, respecting her own needs and also considering the needs of her boss. She offers him an alternative and shows she will compromise.

Another person who has a problem with assertion is Nancy.

When her boss says, "You can cover for Amy while she's on vacation, can't you?" Nancy's response is: "Fine. No problem." His fuzzy question receives her vague answer. Nancy hasn't found out exactly what he expects from her, and her answer doesn't tell him exactly what she's willing—or not willing—to do.

She could answer, assertively: "I'll be glad to take care of Amy's accounts up until the end of the month, if you need me to. But I'll need your okay to get the extra clerical people, and I'll also have to postpone my report to the department a few weeks."

2. *Use "I" not "you" statements.* When you confront someone with "You always . . ." or "You never . . . ," they feel accused and become defensive. Think how you feel when someone says, "You did it wrong," or "You don't understand this." When a person is attacked or accused, he or she will react negatively. To avoid a negative reaction, begin your thought or sentence with "I" instead of "you."

Meg's boss tends to overload her with work. Finally, she confronts him: "You can't expect me to make all those calls, get to the bank, and have the Chicago report typed for you by five o'clock. You don't realize what's involved here. You're not being reasonable." By beginning each sentence with "you" Meg makes the boss feel accused. He's forced to defend himself or attack her back.

Meg could have answered, assertively: "I have only seven hours a day and I can't finish everything. I'd like you to tell me what the high priority jobs are so I can finish those first."

When you begin a sentence with "I" you are more likely to express your ideas and feelings in an honest, unthreatening way. Communication is clearer and more easily accepted when you begin sentences with phrases like:

"I need . . ."

"I would like you to . . ."

"I feel disappointed that . . ."

"I am annoyed by . . ."

"I get confused when you . . ."

"I am not comfortable with . . ."

"I would prefer that you . . ."

Think how your subordinate will respond to being told, "Donna, you're getting sloppy lately. You're making mistakes that could cost you your job. You can't go on like this. You'd better watch it." She will respond in a more useful way if she's told, "Donna, I've noticed a lot of errors in your work lately. I'm sure I don't have to tell you how serious this could be. I'd like to know why you think this is happening and what you could do to improve the situation."

3. *Give feedback.* Repeat the other person's message to be sure you have understood it. When you give orders or make a request of someone, ask him or her to repeat back what you've said to be sure he or she understands fully. Has your boss ever given you a lot of instructions, rushed off to a meeting and left you sitting in a maze, not at all sure what is wanted? Here is how Louise assertively handled a similar situation.

BOSS: Louise, call Bob Carter in Chicago. Tell him I'll try to make the morning plane. Have him get Brenner, Jones, and Black together so we can work on the warehouse deal. I'll need some copies of the storage charges, and I'll also need to go over the correspondence from Williams on the new contract.

LOUISE: Let me make sure I've got this right. First of all, what day are you leaving for Chicago? Which warehouse deal? We have three in the works. Also, how many copies do you want of the storage invoices, and from what year and month? Do you want the whole file on the contract for Williams or just the correspondence for the last few months?

If Louise had not been assertive, she would have simply nodded "Okay, sure," and then tried to guess what he wanted.

She might guess right, or her boss might end up in Chicago with the wrong materials in his briefcase and possibly with a meeting set up on the wrong day.

4. *Be specific.* Spell out exactly the goals and actions you want taken. If you give an order or make a request, you'll get better results by outlining exactly what you want the person to do. Michelle's boss failed to do this. He told her, "You're the the office manager, Michelle, and it's up to you to see that the office personnel get on the ball. Things have been getting very unprofessional around here lately. You'd better start doing something to make some changes around here—fast!"

The boss could have said, assertively: "I've noticed that there's a lot of lateness and absenteeism this month, Michelle. I've also noticed that in spite of my suggestion that you stagger the lunch breaks, there hasn't been one secretary in here between twelve and one. I want you to monitor these areas closely during the next week and give me a written report on both problems. Also, I'd like a written list of suggestions for correcting them. Please give it to me within the next two weeks."

ASSERTIVE TECHNIQUES

Broken Record

Broken record is a technique often used in assertiveness workshops to prevent oneself from being sidetracked by a persistent or persuasive individual. You keep returning to your original statement or thought, and avoid getting hooked or put off course by the other person's arguments. Just repeat, again and again, what you want, without "hearing" the attempts the other person makes to talk you out of something or distract you from your original intent. In the following dialogue, Shirley uses the broken record technique to handle a nagging friend.

JOAN: Shirl, I don't believe you didn't sign up for the cruise this year.

SHIRLEY: Yes, I decided not to go.

JOAN: But why? Didn't you have fun last year? I thought you loved it.

SHIRLEY: Well, I decided I'd skip it this year.

JOAN: Come on. Jim and Mark will be really disappointed if you don't go. They're counting on it.

SHIRLEY: To tell you the truth, I've just decided I don't care to go this year.

JOAN: But why? We were all counting on you. Everyone will be disappointed.

SHIRLEY: I'm sorry about that, but I've really made up my mind not to go.

JOAN: Why? Just give me one good reason. Was it the director? Was it because . . .

SHIRLEY: Joan, I understand how much you want me to go, but I just prefer not to this year.

JOAN: Everyone will think you're a snob.

SHIRLEY: That's possible. They may think that. But I've made up my mind. I'm not going on the cruise this year.

However, don't take the broken record technique too literally. If you totally block out the other person, the tactic is abusive, and you will provoke hostility. That is what happened to Lisa in the following exchange:

LISA: Martin, I'd like you to be on time tonight.

MARTIN: Why? Was I so late the last time?

LISA: I'd like you to be on time tonight.

MARTIN: What's so special about tonight?

LISA: I'd like you to be on time tonight.

MARTIN: I understand. But why should you be so concerned? I'm not always late. What are you worried about?

LISA: I'd like you to be on time tonight.

MARTIN: I heard you the first time! You're beginning to sound like a damned broken record! What is it with you?

LISA: I'd like you to be on time tonight.

MARTIN: (exasperated) I don't believe this! Tell you what. I'll make it easy for you. I won't come at all. Good night!

Fogging

The broken record technique is best when used with fogging. In fogging you show the other person respect and offer them the satisfaction of knowing that they have been heard by acknowledging their position, even agreeing with those points you think are valid, and *then* return to the broken record. In the following conversation fogging and broken record are used by Sandy.

MOTHER: I don't understand why you're going out with Paul again. Why don't you stay home tonight?

SANDY: We made a date, and I'd like to see him tonight.

MOTHER: Don't you think you should get some rest?

SANDY: No, mom. I have plans to go out.

MOTHER: What do you see in him, anyway?

SANDY: I like Paul and I'm seeing him tonight.

MOTHER: I think you should be seeing other men. That's what your sister always did. I don't know why you can't be more like her.

SANDY: It's true, we are very different. Anyway, I'm very fond of Paul, and I'm seeing him tonight.

MOTHER: Your father and I think you could do much better. Paul doesn't even have a steady job.

SANDY: I understand how you and dad feel. And I know you're concerned. I've got to get going now. I have a date.

MOTHER: He's not worthy of you. You're going to ruin your life. You'll be sorry, mark my words.

SANDY: I'm sorry you feel that way, mom. But I happen to really like Paul. We have a date, and now I have to leave.

MOTHER: What do you see in him, anyway? Just tell me that. Is that too much to ask?

SANDY: Mom, I like Paul, and now I really must go.

MOTHER: He's changed you. Look at how cold you are. He's turning you against us.

SANDY: Mom, I love you and dad very much, and I also care for Paul. If you want to, we can talk about it later when there's more time. Now I have to go or I'll be late. Good night, mom. (Sandy then kisses her mother on the cheek and leaves.)

Fogging statements can begin with phrases like:
"You may be right, but . . ."
"I can appreciate how you feel, but . . ."
"I understand your position, but . . ."
"That's a good point you raised, but . . ."
"I can see how that might bother you, but . . ."
"I understand how you feel, but . . ."
This way you acknowledge the other person's feelings and beliefs, but still stick with your position. Remember, the purpose of assertiveness training is to learn how to express your-

self in effective, appropriate ways. It's not simply to get what you want from people. Appropriateness means you show consideration of others. This is how assertiveness is different from aggressiveness; it allows greater honesty and mutual respect. You may not always get what you want, but you'll like yourself for trying. And you'll respect yourself for the way you tried.

It will help if you recall some of the situations in which you found yourself acting unassertively. You can probably recall times when you ended up feeling manipulated or put in an awkward position. Maybe you can remember an occasion when you felt you were being stepped on. At such a time you probably felt inadequate. You lost self-respect. Perhaps you failed to act in your own best interests because you mistakenly believed you had no choice in the matter, or no right to act another way.

But you have more rights than you may be aware of. You have the right:

- To be treated with respect.
- To have your own needs and to state them.
- To put your needs before those of the other person, while considering his or her needs.
- To make requests of another person, accepting the fact that you may be turned down.
- To turn down another person's requests.
- To say no.
- To choose not to explain or justify your actions, or to choose not to make excuses.
- To express your feelings—anger, dissatisfaction, disappointment, affection, satisfaction—and to take responsibility for the consequences.
- To express a contrary opinion.
- To say "I don't understand," and to ask questions.
- To say "I don't know."

- To say "I need more time to think about it."
- To make a mistake and assume the responsibility.
- To recognize your personal rights and to stand up for them.

If you are an appropriately assertive woman, you give and get respect. You take responsibility for the results of your actions. You are firm but not unyielding. An assertive person can take a strong position yet not be rigid. When you are secure in your position and you don't feel threatened, you are open to alternative ideas and solutions, and you will be willing to work out compromises if you need to.

STANDING UP FOR YOUR RIGHTS AT WORK

6

OFFICE CONFRONTATIONS

Assertive techniques are useful in many office situations. You may have to confront a subordinate whose work has been getting worse. Are you going to wait until it becomes more unsatisfactory? Collect all the evidence against him or her and then have him fired? That might be the style of a manager who doesn't want or perhaps doesn't know how to take the time to talk the problem over with the employee.

It's usually better to deal with the problem as soon as you become aware of it, by having an honest and constructive dialogue. The first thing you need to do is pinpoint the problem and the employee's role in it. Then come to an agreement with him or her about how it is going to be solved. In this way the issues will not become distorted by emotional flare-ups or long-term resentment. Good communication is often the responsibility of the boss. It helps maintain an atmosphere of mutual respect and good manager-subordinate relationships.

123

Janice is a division manager for a large manufacturing company. It came to her attention that Larry, one of the salespeople, was falling behind in his accounts. He was late making follow-up calls and his orders were often sloppily done, and full of errors, but Janice handled the problem successfully and assertively.

Step One. She investigated the situation. She checked with his superiors and others in the order department. After she'd gotten all the facts she was ready to plan her approach.

Step Two. She arranged a meeting between herself and Larry. On the phone, she said to him:

JANICE: Larry, I'd like to see you in my office. Right away, unless you're busy. If you can't see me now, then at two this afternoon.

LARRY: Oh, I suppose now is as good as later on.

In arranging the meeting, Janice made it clear what she wanted, and also showed consideration for Larry by allowing him an option. The option was limited, so he couldn't avoid meeting her request. It's a little like the illusion of choice you give a teenager when you ask: "Would you like to clean up your room this afternoon or tomorrow morning?"

Step Three. Janice specified the problem behavior that Larry needed to change:

JANICE: Larry, you had really high totals for the first quarter this year and I'm very satisfied with the way you built up new accounts.

LARRY: Well, that's nice to hear. Thank you.

JANICE: There is one problem, though, and it's serious. When you don't make those follow-up calls, we lose the sales. Also, your orders are done so fast they're not always accurate. We had two overcharges last month because of it. These orders could cost us a lot of money. I'm very concerned about this, Larry.

Janice has described the problem and his role in it precisely. She didn't threaten, but simply stated the real consequences if he doesn't change what he's doing. She was careful to begin their talk with some positive comments about his work. She didn't attack Larry personally, she focused her remarks on his behavior.

LARRY: I'm really sorry about this. I guess I've been letting things pile up and I got behind this quarter. I'll make sure it doesn't happen again.

Step Four. Janice and Larry agreed on a solution that was acceptable to them both.

JANICE: Fine, Larry, but I'll feel better if you can tell me exactly how you can plan to do it. I'd like to talk it over right now, to find out what you could arrange differently so you don't fall behind again.

LARRY: Well, one thing I haven't been doing is keeping my folders out so I can make the calls again each week. I guess I could keep a list, instead of keeping it all in my head.

JANICE: What about time management? Do you think there's any way you could cut down on some of the other things you've been doing? Are they all necessary?

LARRY: I guess I've been spending as much time on the Mickey Mouse accounts as I have on the big ones. I could organize my priorities better.

Janice wasn't satisfied with Larry's vague promise that he'll "make sure it doesn't happen again." She asked him to outline specifically what he intended to do about the situation, and how he expected to do it. She also offered some suggestions.

Step Five. Janice made certain that Larry was in agreement as to what he was supposed to do, and that he understood exactly what was expected of him.

JANICE: Those sound like good ideas, Larry. I'll expect you to start putting them to work right away. You do understand how serious it is to have the orders go out with mistakes on them, don't you?

LARRY: Yes, I do. I wouldn't want to be responsible for losing the division money.

JANICE: Fine. I hope you'll keep up your good work in recruiting new accounts, too, Larry."

Janice ended their talk by making absolutely certain Larry understood what they'd decided. She also gave him a word of encouragement along with a compliment.

Paula, in contrast, handled a similar problem with Carl in an unassertive way. Like Larry, Carl had failed to make follow-up calls and was not careful with the figures in his orders.

PAULA: Carl, there's something important we must talk about.

CARL: Of course. What's wrong?

PAULA: Well, first of all how's your family? Stephanie get over her flu?

CARL: She's fine. Everyone's okay.

PAULA: And the kids? Joshua still doing well in school?

CARL: Fine, everything's fine. Now what's up?

PAULA: How about the addition you were putting on the house? Did you get it finished?

CARL: No, not yet. Now tell me what's wrong.

PAULA: Good, I'm glad everything's going well at home. Oh, yes, your totals for this quarter.

CARL: What about my totals?

PAULA: Frankly, Carl, you're slipping. Maybe you're just losing interest.

CARL: What do you mean? What's the problem?

PAULA: You seem to be dragging your heels. There have been some complaints. You're just not on top of things the way you should be.

CARL: I thought I was doing okay. I thought my orders were high enough.

PAULA: You know you made two serious errors this month. You could lose your job if you keep that up. The company has a strict policy about things like that. You better start shaping up, Carl. I don't know what else to tell you.

CARL: Okay, Paula. I'll try. I'll really try to give it my best shot next month.

PAULA: Good. I knew you'd understand.

Paula and Carl had an unproductive exchange. Paula didn't make it clear what she wanted. Carl didn't really understand what she was asking him to do. They left the discussion with no agreement about what would be done specifically to solve the problem.

You will find it helpful to remember these dos and don'ts

when you are involved in office situations like the ones described:

1. Avoid wasting time getting to the point.
2. Describe the problem and say specifically what your subordinate has been doing that is a problem.
3. Avoid evaluating in general terms, such as "You're slipping."
4. Avoid depersonalizing statements such as "the company won't tolerate . . ." or "the company's policy is . . ." Janice's show of personal concern probably had a greater positive effect on Larry than Paula's remark to Carl about "policy."
5. Be specific about the behavior change you want: "Get your orders in with no errors," instead of "Start shaping up."
6. Be sure your subordinate understands the problem and what you expect from him or her in the way of a change.
7. Go over the specific steps he or she plans to take to effect the changes you've agreed on.
8. Avoid threatening the person with dire consequences if the problem isn't solved.
9. Describe realistically the troublesome results of the problem behavior: "Making errors on your orders is costing the company a lot of money. It could affect your position here if it keeps up."

GIVING AND RECEIVING ORDERS

As a woman you may have been frustrated trying to get your ideas or messages heard in a male-dominated organization. Perhaps your male colleagues are able to drive their points home with a few well-placed remarks. But you have had to work twice as hard to convince others of your point. If you come into a position of authority with such experiences you might continue to wield your authority in the same heavy-handed way, not realizing that you no longer need to do it. Sometimes a woman executive who is used to struggling to make her points will be particularly abrasive and authoritarian when she deals with male subordinates or male peers. She isn't out to win a popularity contest, of course. But it's important to be aware that if you want to continue moving up, you will need the respect of your co-workers, and this means treating both peers and subordinates with consideration and respect.

There are several helpful rules for giving orders or assigning tasks:

1. Be clear in your own mind exactly what you want the other person to do.
2. Be sure that the person you are giving the order to is capable of doing what you ask and within the time you allow for it.
3. State your orders simply and clearly. Make clear which items have higher priority and which are less important.
4. Make sure your subordinate has understood. Ask him or her to repeat back your instructions, so you can be sure that he or she knows exactly what you expect.

The way you give an order will test your credibility as a manager. Use a firm tone of voice so your listener will know you expect your request to be carried out. Avoid asking in an apologetic way, or weakening your order with expressions like: "Do you think you could have this ready for me by tomorrow?" "I wonder if you wouldn't mind making copies of this for me." Instead, use more definite expression, like: "I'd like you to have this ready for me by tomorrow." "Please make copies of this for me."

Giving your orders in a direct, firm but friendly way will

gain the respect and cooperation of your subordinates. As long as you are clear in your own mind that the orders are well thought out and will be followed, others will respond in kind. Sometimes women managers fall into the habit of giving orders in a brusque military style, because they feel uncomfortable making requests. Other times they may give too many small, overly detailed orders, like a schoolteacher, because they have not developed the skill of making direct requests. If you feel either of these applies to you, it may help to practice giving simple, direct orders to a friend, until you are comfortable with it.

Judy is a manager in a small company. One day she needed to send Mark, a stock clerk, to the printer. She was careful to give him the orders clearly, and then get enough feedback from him to be sure he understood.

JUDY: Mark, I want you to go to the printer. You can finish shelving that stock when you get back. This has to be done this afternoon.

MARK: Okay.

JUDY: This is the new requisition form. We'll need three thousand of them before the end of the month. Here are two stock samples. Find out what the cost would be for each one. If the difference is under a hundred dollars for the tinted stock, have him use that. If it's more than a hundred, tell him to use the white. Ask for Frank.

MARK: All right. No problem.

JUDY: Wait. Do you know who our printer is?

MARK: Oh, I was going to ask Peggy.

JUDY: Get a pen. I'll give you the address. It's Arcade Printers, 1200 Canal Street.

MARK: Okay, I got it.

JUDY: Mark, before you go, I want to be sure I haven't left anything out, so go over it again with me.

MARK: Sure. Arcade Printers, 1200 Canal Street. Three thousand copies before the end of the month either on this white stock or on the blue stock, depending on which is cheaper.

JUDY: Not quite, Mark. We know the white will be cheaper.

MARK: Oh, right. Sorry. We go with the blue only if it's not more than one hundred dollars over the white. And, let's see, . . . who was I supposed to ask for?

JUDY: Frank. Write that down. If he's not there, see Oscar. Please leave right now, before they close for lunch.

MARK: Okay. Will do.

All bosses aren't as cautious or as organized as Judy. Bill is a harried, disorganized executive who gives rapid-fire orders, with no realistic idea of how long each job takes and no indication of which jobs get priority. At some point, if you work in a high-powered company, you may have found yourself in a situation like Irene, Bill's assistant.

BILL: Irene, check with accounting and bring me this month's figures on disbursements against the Cal-tron account. I must have them before I leave today. I'll want to see the promotion costs for the Rainer project as soon as you finish them. Better get on that right now. Oh, yes, the contract with Dynamic—as soon as you have it retyped with the new distribution clause, I'll sign it. Call the lawyer for the wording. That's urgent. It's got to get out today. And don't forget to send a telex to Marco about the change in the production schedule. Better do that right now.

Thirty minutes later, Bill reappears in Irene's office.

BILL: Irene, drop whatever you're doing! Get over to the credit department and find out what's holding them up on the Rainer account. Tomorrow is our deadline on that deal. By the way, you've taken care of those other things, haven't you?

If you were Irene, how would you react? Apologize profusely and burst into tears? Race around inefficiently, trying to get everything done? Lose your temper at him and tell him he's impossible? Or handle him assertively and unemotionally, as Irene does.

IRENE: Bill, before you go, I see that we've got two hours before you have to leave for the airport. In that amount of time I can't possibly do all the things you've asked. I suggest you decide which items take priority and I'll finish those first. The new contract will take me about an hour to get ready, and I'll need at least another hour to get the Rainer promotion figures for you. That doesn't leave much time to get the Cal-tron figures or the telex to Marco.

BILL: Oh. Let's see. You're right. Sorry, I didn't realize the time was so short. Let Lois finish the contract and get the Cal-tron figures. I'll tell Gary to send the telex. You work on the promotion costs. That's priority.

IRENE: I think that'll work out fine, Bill.

Irene has made a clear and simple statement of what Bill can expect of her within a given time period. She is setting time limits and asking him to be specific about priorities. She is able to get the important jobs done.

ASKING FOR A RAISE

Talent and competence alone aren't enough if you want to move up in business. Good strategy and assertiveness are essential. You need to make yourself visible to the executives who can help you. And you must ask for higher-paid, more responsible positions if you want them. When you are ready to ask for a raise or promotion, you may find it helpful to take the following steps.

1. *Make a list of all your skills and responsibilities.* How have you expanded your responsibilities since you started your position? Profit is the bottom line in any company. How have you helped your organization to make a profit? Have you improved any procedures? Cut costs? Increased sales? Come up with any new product ideas? Have you taken over responsibility for your boss? Done something to make her or him look good? If you have, he or she should be willing to support you in your request.

2. *Do some research on salaries.* If you aren't sure how much you should ask for, find out what the going rate is for someone in your position. You can check ads in newspapers. Ask co-workers and friends and other people in the field. Salary surveys are constantly being published that will help you judge what's appropriate. (See page 282, The Job Interview.") Professional organizations usually provide salary guidelines. You will probably find the American Management Association's *Salary Survey* in your personnel department.

Have clear in your mind the specific amount you will ask for. That can be per year, week, or month. If you name a specific figure you're more likely to get the increase amount you want. Remember, small token raises are handed out automatically by many companies every year—don't confuse this with asking for, and getting, a raise.

3. *Make an appointment to see your boss.* Before you go to discuss a raise with your boss, organize your mind clearly, so you'll be prepared to deal with any objections. Your homework prepares you for whatever may come your way. It's important to be assertive, but not pushy. Many women tend to be either nonassertive or too aggressive. You should be direct and confident.

Before you talk to the boss, ask yourself: What have I done? What skills do I have? What are my job responsibilities?

What are the areas where I've assumed more responsibility in the organization? How have I benefited the company?

Remember, raises aren't given on the basis of need; they are based on your responsibility and performance. Your salary reflects how valuable you are to the organization. Also keep in mind that most salaries are negotiable. There's no such thing as a frozen salary. Companies constantly stretch their salary scale for deserving talent.

When you talk to your supervisor, approach her or him confident that your work deserves some reward. Your request will be more effective if she or he sees that you believe in your own worth, and if you can point to specific contributions you've made.

4. *Timing is important.* If raises are handed out in February, don't ask in March. Also, success makes people generous. They want to share their good fortune. A good time to ask for a raise is when your boss has just had a significant success, or if you have recently completed a successful high-visibility program or in some way brought positive attention to yourself.

During your talk with your boss, don't threaten to quit—or anything else. Threats only antagonize people and make it hard for them to agree with you. Never make any threat unless you're prepared to carry it out. You will do well to convey the attitude that you very much enjoy your job and that you definitely want to stay with the company, but that you would like to discuss adjusting your salary to fit your added responsibilities. When you leave the interview give your superior a copy of the memo that outlines what you've done. It will refresh his or her memory later.

Remember that raises are given to keep employees happy. If the management of your company thinks you're content to get one-third less than a man who does the same amount of work, they'll leave it that way. But it's more expensive for them to hire and train a replacement for an unhappy employee who quits than it is to give a good manager the raise she deserves.

THE LANGUAGE OF POWER AND AUTHORITY

If you were a Japanese woman living in Japan, the language you'd be speaking would be different from your male counterpart's. It would still be Japanese, but with distinct differences. You would be using special verb forms and sentences composed in supercourteous syntax in order to convey respect. This would be considered proper usage by Japanese women and people in subordinate roles. There is literally a language of authority and a language of subservience.

If we listen—and look—closely, we can also find differences in the English language, though on a more subtle level, that separate the powerful from the powerless, and similarly the men from the women.

Let's eavesdrop on a conversation between a male bank vice-president and a woman junior officer while they wait in line at the executive dining room:

"Good afternoon, Miss Davis."

"Oh, my goodness, Mr. Golden. Hello! Why, I didn't notice. How *are* you. Oh, my, isn't this a long line? It seems like it's taking forever, doesn't it? I mean it really is kind of slow, isn't it?" (She looks up at him inquiringly.)

(Looking off into space) "It does seem to be moving more slowly than usual."

"Boy, does it ever! And here I thought I'd be saving time coming here instead of going out. Sure looks like I made the wrong move, doesn't it?"

(Looking over the tables) "Ummm, yes."

"Oh, well, you know what they say: 'Patience is a virtue.' Except I don't think it's one of mine. I mean, I really just hate to wait on long lines. For anything, but especially for food. You know, I mean especially when you're hungry."

(Silence. Miss Davis looks down at her tray, moves her silverware around. Mr. Golden stands still, hands clasped in front of him, continuing to stare off into space.)

"It does become sort of frustrating after a while, doesn't it? I mean you kind of feel like . . ."

(Interrupting) "You can move ahead now, Miss Davis."

"Oh, yes. Of course." (Smiling at him) "Gosh, what a relief!"

"Ummm."

They are signaled by the waiter, and Mr. Golden moves away.)

"Enjoy your lunch, Miss Davis."

"Oh, yes. Thank you very much. You, too, Mr. Golden. Have a good day. Bye-bye, now."

The speech of a person in authority reflects his or her power. But regardless of position, whenever a man and woman communicate the stage is set for a verbal power play. The moves, some nonverbal, usually go unnoticed. Look at how hard Miss Davis tries to engage Mr. Golden, to catch and hold his attention, to fill the gaps of silence. He remains poised while she shifts nervously. He stares beyond her while she watches his face hoping for a sign of recognition, of agreement or approval. And how do you imagine she feels when she reaches her table and sits down?

"Oh, God! I feel so embarrassed! What was I so nervous about? Why did I have to talk so much? He must think I'm a real lightweight!"

Have you ever found yourself coming away from an interaction like that? Maybe you've had the feeling of having been talked down to, of feeling unimportant—as if what you had to say was not being listened to. You can't put your finger on what was said, but you're somehow left feeling ineffectual or just stupid. Like Miss Davis, you've probably been using the communication style of the powerless. The style that most women have become accustomed to, and a style that immediately places them in a nondominant role.

Let's take a closer look at the differences between men's and women's styles of communication.

Men touch women more than women touch men during conversation.

Women try harder to please men in conversation.

Women make their voices go up in a questioning tone, as if they're asking for approval.

Women soften their statements with phrases like, "I suppose," "sort of," "you know," "I think."

Women's speech tends to be more polite and more emotional in quality.

Men's speech is more direct, more informative.

Men use silences and interruptions to assert power.

Men will often talk down to a woman, as if she were a child or someone simply not worthy of their attention.

Some men may use "hon" or "sweetie," casually.

Men may look away, tune you out, while you're talking to them.

Women's speech frequently lacks credibility. If a woman doesn't feel authoritative, she doesn't sound authoritative. As a result, she will not be viewed as an authority and will fail to be placed in a position of authority. She's caught in a vicious cycle. Because she's forced to try harder, she adopts the language of the subservient.

Things to Check for

Do you pay closer attention to the man you are talking to than he does to you?

Are you uncomfortable with silent gaps in the conversation?

Do you often have to repeat what you've said because he doesn't answer?

Do you find yourself searching the other person's face for signs of approval, and switch the conversation if you sense disapproval?

Do you smile a lot more than he does? Laugh a lot more?

Do you hear yourself apologizing frequently?

How often do you say, "Do you think that . . ." when you want to make a suggestion?

Start monitoring yourself when you're in conversation with men. When you learn to recognize the subtle power plays you'll be able to counter them by not responding in the expected way. With practice you'll be able to spot the weaknesses in your language and start to develop a communication style with more power.

7 RISK TAKING

Many women grow up protected from failure and loss. As we saw earlier, women don't have the experience of playing the kind of games that men do. Competitive games teach boys to take loss in stride, that there's always a next time. Women often tend to avoid situations where risk is involved because of their inexperience in competing and their fear of failure. They see failure as irrevocable. They can't say, as a man does, "I win some, I lose some."

If this is true of you, you may hesitate to take risks because you see risk as a chance to lose something or to get hurt. You may become anxious when you aren't absolutely sure of the outcome. A man, on the other hand, is more likely to see risk as a chance to win something, to prove himself, or to gain something. Calculating a risk is a skill that can be learned (see "Decision Making and Problem Solving," in Chapter Fifteen). A woman who is afraid to take risks will have difficulty making decisions, which would surely keep her from functioning in an executive position.

In upper management just performing well in a routine job isn't enough. Many companies reward innovation. In such cases, promotion often comes from taking visible risks. For example, risks you, as a manager, can take are reorganizing your staff; bringing someone in from outside the corporation to fill a key post under you; or creating a subgroup from a larger group in the company. You might abolish a system set up by your predecessor and institute a new procedure. Much of risk taking involves keen calculation. Often a shrewd manager will take a "risk" but actually know the outcome. Sometimes a risk can look daring when it actually isn't. But to climb in management you have to look like someone who's willing to take a gamble. Anyone who takes a risk and succeeds develops credibility.

For some women, learning to take even a small risk is difficult at first. A very competent woman often will avoid making changes on the job even though she sees they could be beneficial. A simple thing like changing an office procedure may seem too risky to her. She might remain in the same secure, boring job for fear of the risks involved in trying a more challenging one.

In the following case histories you will see how four women were able to overcome their fears of risk taking and take an active role in changing the course of their careers.

AFRAID TO LEAVE A SAFE JOB: MICHELLE

Michelle came from a comfortable home in the suburbs of Chicago. She'd gone to a design school and at first was interested in decorating and design. She had a feel for colors and fabrics, and gravitated toward a job in a small textile firm. There she worked as assistant to the production manager. She enjoyed the general atmosphere and was highly respected by her employer and co-workers. It was an old, established firm;

the owner was like a father to her. She felt like she was part of a big family.

Eventually she was offered a position as production manager in a merchandising department of a new textile company. It meant a substantial increase in salary, but greater responsibility and challenge as well. Michelle couldn't make up her mind whether to risk accepting the new position or stay where she was. She stayed up nights worrying, and kept putting off giving her prospective employers any final decision.

PROBLEM: She was afraid to leave a safe job for a situation that would further her career, because she was afraid of taking risks.

Solution

A. Make a List of Risks Involved

I asked Michelle to make a list of all the risks involved and how she viewed them. She drew up the following:

1. It's a new company, and in a new company there's always a chance the firm won't make it.
2. I may not make any new friends as good as the ones I have here. It'll take me forever to make new friends.
3. If I don't do well I'll never get another job as good as the one I have now.
4. I'll have to deal with a larger number of subordinates and I may have a problem with that.
5. The new people won't like me.
6. I'll have to take on the responsibility of making decisions for the department and I may not do well.

I asked Michelle to separate the real risks from the imagined ones. She decided the real risks were:

1. It's a new company, and in a new company there's always a chance the firm won't make it.

4. I'll have to deal with a larger number of subordinates and I may have a problem with that.
6. I'll have to take on the responsibility of making decisions for the department and I may not do well.

B. Evaluate Self-talk

She realized that the imagined risks were based on irrational statements she was making to herself:

2. It'll take me forever to make new friends. If I do make friends I'll never be as close to them as I am to the ones I have here.
3. If I don't do well I won't get another job as good as the one I have now.
5. The new people won't like me.

We took each irrational statement and challenged it with a rational one:

IRRATIONAL	RATIONAL
2. I may not make any new friends.	2. It's interesting to make new friends. I may meet some interesting new people.
3. If I don't do well on this job I may never get another one as good as the one I have now.	3. People were satisfied with me in my other job. I was offered this job. Certainly other people will offer me jobs. Two companies want me; certainly others will.
5. The new people won't like me.	5. People like me, so these people will too. I know how to make friends.

After Michelle read over the column of rational statements

she had written, she began to develop a different view of the job situation. As a result many of her tearful and negative feelings soon gave way to positive ones.

C. Use GPE for Risk Taking

Since Michelle had high anxiety about taking risks, I suggested she build a GPE hierarchy for risk taking. First she made a list of anxiety-provoking situations involving risk, and arranged them according to their SUD rating, from least disturbing to most disturbing:

SUD	SITUATION
30	Ordering tickets to a show before the reviews
50	Putting a bet on a horse or ball game
60	Assigning a trainee to a job in the dye room because someone's sick
70	Telling the boss the company can take an order for a certain type of merchandise because she expects it to be delivered
80	Ordering a lot of plastic fabric for next year on information that plastics will go up in price because of the oil shortage
90	Telling her landlord she's leaving her apartment in a month because she's been promised a much nicer one

When Michelle got home, she went into her room where she knew she wouldn't be disturbed. She made sure the phone was turned off, changed into something comfortable, and relaxed on her bed. She took three long deep breaths, exhaling slowly, and then began muscle relaxation exercises. When she completed them she deepened her relaxation by picturing herself in a beautiful, peaceful setting in the country. Then she was ready to imagine the scenes in her hierarchy. She started with the scene she had rated 30 SUD. She imagined it for about eight seconds. She felt little or no anxiety, and so moved on to the second scene. She noticed her anxiety level rise as she imagined herself betting on a horse—not to the 50 she had anticipated, but to around 30. She returned to relaxing and to the calming scene for ten seconds, until she was down to about 10. Then she repeated the second scene. This time the increase was hardly noticeable. She erased the scene from her mind, relaxed, and went on to the third scene.

It took Michelle four sessions to complete the hierarchy. She had to repeat the last two scenes for a few days before she finally got comfortable with them.

As she was doing this I had her try the first two scenes in real life. At each session she came up with risks she was willing to take. Because they were small ones she got in the habit of taking risks. She told herself taking risks makes life more interesting.

Each time she took a risk she praised herself, with statements like, "I'm handling this well"; "I enjoy doing this." Her first risk in business was deciding that the firm should switch back to a previous supplier who had been more cooperative than the present one.

Then I had Michelle make a new friend; that was another kind of risk.

She joined a club, one she had hesitated joining before, because the members were more worldly than she.

She called up someone she didn't know too well and asked them to have lunch.

She took reasonable risks, where she was most likely to win. After each risk, whether she succeeded or not, she complimented herself on her initiative, and her willingness to try something new. "Good! You're bringing more interesting things into your life." If it was a real risk: "This is an opportunity to get something you don't have now."

Finally Michelle was able to leave her old job and accept the new one confidently, with very little anxiety.

DEPENDENT: KATHLEEN

Kathleen finished two years of college and then got married. In the first years of her marriage she worked while her husband finished dental school. Then she had three children. While they were growing up she was very active in their lives. She was involved in the Brownies and was a Cub Scout den mother. When her children were grown, her husband had a heart attack and couldn't work. She found herself in financial trouble. Her husband was a strong man who had protected her from the real world. After the heart attack she found she couldn't lean on him anymore. She was confused and frightened and knew that it was up to her to supplement the family's income. They had spent a great deal of their savings educating their children, and the rest of the money they had put aside was spent on doctors' bills. The children were off on their own and she didn't want to be a burden to them. She used to type well, but now her speed was down to thirty words per minute. She knew she should go back to school to sharpen her old skills and acquire new ones if she wanted to be proficient enough to compete with young people coming out of school.

PROBLEM: She was insecure and afraid to go out into the world.

Solution

A. Evaluate Self-talk

Kathleen was making some irrational statements to herself that were the basis for her fears. She had to substitute rational statements for the irrational messages she was giving herself.

IRRATIONAL	RATIONAL
1. I can't promote myself.	1. I've promoted myself in other things. I promoted

myself when I had to for the children. When I wanted to get things for the Cub Scouts and Brownies I promoted myself. I can do the same thing here. I can learn assertive skills.

2. I'm too old to go back to school.

2. People can learn at any age.

3. I can't get a job by myself; I need help picking out a dress.

3. I'll find out how you get a job and I'll go about doing it. I don't expect to be president of the company in the beginning. I don't *have* to get the first job I apply for, I'll just practice until I'm comfortable.

4. I won't be able to run my household and work.

4. The world won't fall apart if my house isn't as perfect as it's always been.

5. Nobody wants an older person working for them.

5. I have interpersonal skills a younger person hasn't. I'll find a corporation that will value the additional skills an older woman has to offer.

6. The business world is too complicated; I could never learn to function in it.

6. I can find the information I need. I can get the training I need.

7. I haven't worked for sixteen years. It's too late to start.

7. I'll have to brush up on my skills or acquire new ones.

B. Build New Skills

I suggested she do some research about the business world;

read up on jobs available and where to find them, in magazines like *Savvy, Working Woman,* or *Ms.*; and freshen up the skills she'd need. She registered for courses so she could improve her typing and steno until they were up to eighty words per minute.

I agreed that reentry probably meant she'd have to start at the beginning. She couldn't expect to start higher up; she'd have to find a place that fit her accomplishments. (See "The Reentry Woman," page 266.)

C. Make a List of Personal Assets

Then, at my suggestion, Kathleen made a list of her assets. What she liked about herself; things she'd done. I had her add to them and reread them every day. She made a little booklet of them. Some of her entries were:

- I'm good at handling people.
- I was one of the best mothers in the Brownies; they always called on me.
- When Mike had his heart attack I handled the family well. I was very good in the emergency situation.
- I organize my home well; I have a very organized household and everything runs efficiently.
- I'm very good at problem solving. My children's friends always come to me to solve their problems. My son discusses his business problems with me and he takes my advice.

D. Use GPE for Independence

Since it was very frightening for Kathleen to think of standing on her own, I suggested she build a GPE hierarchy for independence.

SUD	SITUATION
30	Buying something for herself with no one else's advice

40	Planning an overnight trip on her own
50	Taking a volunteer job for a local hospital or library
60	Enrolling in a business management course
70	Replying to some want ads and going on interviews
80	Getting a part-time job
90	Getting a full-time job

She followed the procedure for relaxing and exposing herself in imagery to each of the scenes on the hierarchy. When she succeeded in imagining the last item with only slight anxiety, she was ready to try them in real life. The last two items on the hierarchy required more time and effort. Soon she was feeling more self-confident. She began to see herself in a different light. She reported to me whenever she had a chance to do something independently. Every time she did, she reinforced herself with praise: "This is a new part of me I'm discovering." "Wonderful, I like it; I like me!"

E. Learn Assertive Skills

After some assertiveness training—learning to initiate conversation, saying no, making requests, and so forth—Kathleen began to change. She became more confident and more assertive. She felt more comfortable making new friends in her business management course; she went to lunch with them and learned from their experiences. Her self-image began to change. She was more self-assured. She began to identify with people in the business world. She started viewing the outside world in a different way and was stimulated by the challenge. She started realizing that she was interesting to other people. Her tone, her manner changed—she even walked straighter, she held her head high. She looked much younger. She realized you don't have to be a breed apart to make it in the business world. There were a lot of women like her.

LEAVING HOME: JENNIFER

Jennifer was raised in a small Pennsylvania town. After she finished college, where she got a degree in journalism, she returned to her hometown to work on the newspaper there. She was a staff reporter, a good writer, and worked very hard. After about four years she began to get a little bored with the routine stories she generally covered. She wrote a six-part series about local factory workers, which attracted the attention of an editor of a Philadelphia paper. Suddenly she found herself with a job offer from a major daily with a nationwide circulation. She was thrilled by the opportunity, but at the same time she was terrified at the thought of leaving home: her parents, brothers and sisters, friends, all the people she felt secure with. It frightened her to think about living away from home in a big city where she didn't know anybody. But she knew if she wanted to succeed in journalism she'd have to break her ties to home. She was confident she could handle the new job, and eager to take it on, but she knew she'd turn it down unless she could overcome her fears.

PROBLEM: She was afraid to leave home and the security of a safe job, and go to a big town and a new position.

Solution

A. Evaluate Self-talk

I first suggested that Jennifer evaluate her messages to herself. She was pretty confident about her abilities on the job. What she did worry about was being alone and meeting new people socially. Her fears centered around some negative and irrational messages she was giving herself:

1. I'll have a terrible time.
2. I'll never make new friends.
3. I'll be alone all the time; it will be unbearable.

4. I don't know how to take care of myself.
5. I'll never be able to run an apartment by myself.
6. I'll miss my family. They'll grow distant from me.

IRRATIONAL	RATIONAL
1. I'll have a terrible time.	1. I'll be doing interesting things. I'll be able to do *more* interesting things.
2. I'll never make new friends.	2. I've made friends before; I will again. I can look up old friends from college. I'll be working with interesting new people.
3. I'll be alone; it will be unbearable.	3. True, at first I will be, but I'll be meeting lots of new people and from among them I'll be able to make friends as soon as I want to.
4. I don't know how to take care of myself.	4. It's about time I learned to take care of myself. This will be a good opportunity.
5. I'll never be able to run an apartment by myself.	5. I can always get some help with the heavy work. And I'll learn to handle the rest.
6. I'll miss my family. They'll grow distant from me.	6. Yes, I will, but I can call them on the phone and visit them. Our visits will be special and may bring us even closer. Besides, I'll have plenty of other things to do.
7. I won't have my mother to help me make my deci-	7. That's true, and it may be good for me. I may find

sions. It will be devastating.

that I'm doing things *I* want to do, rather than things she thinks I should do. I've got to grow up sometime.

B. Learn Conversational Skills

I also recommended that Jennifer learn some Conversational Skills to make new friends. I suggested she read Barbara Walters' *How to Talk with Practically Anybody About Practically Anything*.

C. Use GPE

Jennifer still had a great deal of anxiety about the situation. I asked her what her fears centered around and she said they concerned mostly:

1. being away from home
2. not being able to make new friends
3. being alone

She built the following hierarchy combining being away from home, and being alone:

SUD	SITUATION
20	Going to a local resort beach alone for the day
30	Going to a town 300 miles away with two friends for the week
40	Spending a weekend alone at a vacation spot
50	Spending two weeks away on vacation, 600 miles from home, with a good friend
60	Going to a town 300 miles from home and spending a weekend by herself
70	Going to Philadelphia for three days with a friend

| 90 | Going to Philadelphia alone for two days |
| 100 | Spending a week in Philadelphia by herself |

She next exposed herself to a hierarchy for making new friends:

SUD	SITUATION
10	Starting a conversation with an out-of-town visitor in the newspaper office where she works
20	Talking to a stranger in line at the airport at her hometown
30	Making conversation with the person next to her on the flight to Philadelphia
40	Phoning a friend of a friend in Philadelphia, whom she was told to look up, and visiting her at home
50	Introducing herself to a woman reporter on her new job, and making conversation
60	Introducing herself to a male reporter at the new job, and striking up a conversation
70	Asking a woman colleague at her new job to have lunch
80	Inviting two people from her new job to her house for dinner
90	Introducing herself to a stranger at a cocktail party at her boss's house
100	Inviting a new friend to go sightseeing with her for a weekend trip to New York City

Whenever possible, after she succeeded in imagining an item on the hierarchy without anxiety, she tried exposing herself to the same situation in real life.

D. Create a Personal Image of the Future
Jennifer also used imagery so she could feel more confident

about going to a new place and finding a new life-style. She imaged herself in her new job, in the new office, with new people. She also imaged other aspects of her life: What her new apartment would look like; the friends she would have, and how they would spend their time; the shops, restaurants and discos, and other places to explore in Philadelphia.

E. Practice Behavior in Imagery

After she had rehearsed meeting new people in imagery, we role played situations in the office. She practiced meeting a new person and what she'd say to them. She role played going to a cocktail party.

Jennifer was soon able to accept the job offer and move to Philadelphia. By the time therapy was concluded she'd made some very good friends.

Then, whenever other things came up, we took them one by one and did them in imagery. For instance, she had to cover the mayor's news conference, and she was unsure about her ability to handle it. She got an image of herself amid the excitement and bustle of the mayor's office. She saw herself as a competent professional among a group of other big-city reporters and media people. She used positive thoughts like: "I'm really enjoying this. This is great fun, and a challenge to my abilities."

YOU CAN'T WIN 'EM ALL—CONTENDING WITH DISAPPOINTMENT:

Wendy was only twenty-nine, and in less than a year she had worked her way up to buyer of ladies sportswear for a very large retail chain. She was extremely energetic and ambitious, and was seen as a rising star in the company. Then she had her first disappointment: She overestimated the popularity of a beach top, and the firm's warehouses were heavily overstocked with it at the end of the season. Even when they reduced the price to below cost at the company's outlet stores, they couldn't move the merchandise. As she became painfully aware of the mounting losses Wendy constantly berated herself for her "unforgivable mistake." She began placing smaller orders and choosing only standard items. She blamed herself for being inadequate as a buyer, and doubted her decision-making ability. She saw herself as a failure. Her self-confidence was so shattered that she was considering quitting her job and moving out of state. She became socially withdrawn, and by the time I saw her, was in a serious state of depression. She couldn't see anything positive about herself, her life, or her future.

PROBLEM: When she took a chance and it didn't turn out well, she felt that nothing she would do would ever succeed. She lost confidence in her own ability to make decisions.

Solution

A. Evaluate Self-talk

I first suggested Wendy examine her statements to herself that accompanied her feelings of anxiety. She was persistently making negative comments to herself. Her list was:

1. I can't ever make the right decisions.
2. I never seem to win at things.
3. I know I'll mess up again.
4. I guess I don't have any talent for merchandising.
5. I just got my job through luck.
6. I'll never live this down.
7. Everybody will know what a flop I am.

Wendy then challenged her irrational messages with rational ones:

IRRATIONAL	RATIONAL
1. I can't ever make the right decisions.	1. Just because I made one mistake doesn't mean I'm a failure.
2. I never seem to win at things.	2. I didn't stop to weigh all the consequences when I decided.
3. I know I'll mess up again.	3. We learn from our mistakes, more than from our successes.
4. I guess I don't have any talent for merchandising. I just got my job through luck.	4. I got where I am on merit, not luck.
5. I'll never live this down.	5. One mistake isn't the end of the world. Everybody makes mistakes.
6. Everybody will know what a flop I am.	6. The higher up you are in business, the more you gamble. You win some, you lose some. My boss made plenty of mistakes, too.

B. Use Thought-stopping

Because Wendy found herself dwelling on negative, unrealistic thoughts, I asked her to use thought-stopping. Whenever she found herself ruminating over negative thoughts, she said to herself: Stop! Switch! and substituted a positive, rational statement. She then reinforced the positive statement by imagining herself in a pleasant scene—in her case, lying on a yacht in the Caribbean, with lovely blue water all around her.

C. Make a List of Personal Assets

I then asked Wendy to evaluate herself realistically by

making a list of all her accomplishments and assets. Her one big failure had affected her feelings about herself in her personal as well as business life. She had to remind herself of her many competencies and skills. But since she was so depressed, she had trouble getting in touch with anything positive about herself. So I asked her to make a list in the past: what she *used* to do well, *used* to like or *used* to enjoy. When she finished the list, she could see that it was really quite impressive:

> I get along well with my subordinates at work.
> I was promoted from assistant to buyer in a year.
> I'm considerate of friends and co-workers.
> My boss said I was the best buyer he's had in sportswear.
> I'm a sensitive listener.
> I had scholarships in college.
> My social life is excellent; I have many friends.

I asked her to keep the list by her, and to continue adding to it every day, with positive self-statements about everyday activities. Eventually she had a booklet, and began to have good feelings about herself again.

D. Use GPE for Failing and Losing

Wendy had high anxiety about failure and loss, so I asked her to build a GPE hierarchy for failing and losing:

SUD	SITUATION
10	Presenting a promotion idea at a meeting and having it ignored
20	Choosing an inappropriate display ad for her department that is rejected, and one for cosmetics is substituted by the store.
30	Choosing an assistant who turns out to be inefficient

40	Ordering merchandise that arrives too late for the season
50	Failing to order enough of a certain popular item, and consequently running out of stock in midseason
60	Being told by a supplier that he's selling to a competitor of hers and will no longer sell to her company
70	Applying for a job in a big department, and when its budget is cut, ending up in an unimportant department, with less than what she had
80	Being turned down when she asks for a raise
90	Leaving her job for another company, where she doesn't work out and can't handle the job

She practiced relaxation exercises and was able to complete the first three items on the hierarchy in just one session. By the fifth session she was successful in imagining the most difficult scene on the hierarchy without anxiety. By reducing her anxiety about failure, she was able to feel more positive about the future and see that there were many options available to her.

E. Learn Risk Taking

Wendy needed to learn to calculate a risk. She had picked a beach top that was too highly styled for the customers of her medium-priced chain. She had picked it because she liked it, not stopping to consider if it was a good calculated risk. She had not thought it through but had made a snap decision. Wendy needed to learn to evaluate the possibilities that would make a good risk and a bad risk so she could be more confident in her decisions.

She went through the steps that she had neglected going through earlier when she had made her decision on the beach top. She asked questions and researched both positive and negative aspects of placing the order. The positive aspects were:

1. It's very attractive.
2. Saks Fifth Avenue is carrying it in their their boutique.
3. The supplier will deliver it on time.
4. I like the way it looks; it's something I'd buy.

The negative aspects were:

1. It's a high-priced item and this is a medium-priced chain.
2. It's highly styled, and this chain goes to local towns where people don't dress in high style.
3. You have to be a certain age and have a good figure to wear it—it won't have mass appeal.
4. It's a boutique item, not a chain store item.

Wendy could see her decision was not a good calculated risk. If you, like Wendy, think you need practice in decision making, you'll find more information in Chapter Fifteen.

8

PASSIVITY

Because of the way they were raised, many women tend to wait passively to be taken care of or to have their needs attended to. As a result they don't make the effort to develop their own strengths or skills in ways that would enable them to function independently. For example, they don't create long-range career plans. This attitude may be so ingrained that even when a woman does accomplish something she fails to acknowledge that she was responsible for it. She develops a sense that things "just happen" to her. She thinks: "Someone else did it," or "Someone else will do it for me."

To know if you are one of these women make a list of the most important events that have happened to you in your life. How many do you honestly feel you were responsible for?

As a child you may not have been rewarded, the way a boy is rewarded, for independent accomplishments. As a result, you discount your own strengths. Over the years this gradually leads to a passive attitude toward the world. Discounting your own strengths, initiative and involvement in your accomplishments works against you, and the end result is a firm conviction that you cannot influence your own life. You need someone else to do things for you, or you need luck. Passivity eventually becomes a habit, ingrained in your thinking.

To break that negative thinking, you first need to become aware that your "helplessness" is not based on fact, but on a belief about yourself that comes from your conditioning. You may have learned when you were a little girl that by taking a passive, helpless role, by being sweet and compliant, you would have your needs taken care of by others. You are actually competent and capable, but fail to acknowledge your own strengths because the major events in your life—your educational choices, your marriage, your divorce, your job— seem to have occurred without your initiating any action.

THE CINDERELLA SYNDROME: CAROLE

Carole and her two older brothers were raised in a comfortable split-level home in suburban Westchester County. In school Carole was popular with her classmates. She was a pretty girl, pleasant and easy to get along with. Her parents adored her. She had always been close to her mother, helped her keep an immaculate home, make imaginative meals, and see that the men in the family were taken care of. Her father, sitting at the head of the table, always beamed when Carole served one of her pies for dessert. "That's the mark of a real woman," he'd say proudly, and she'd blush.

Both of her brothers went to universities out of state, but there was no talk of college for Carole during her senior year of high school. After she graduated it seemed like the only expectation her parents had of her was that she keep her lady-like charm. She'd been a good student, but didn't object to stopping her schooling. She passively accepted whatever plans—or nonplans—her parents had for her. One night during a commercial on the *Merv Griffin Show* her mother mentioned that if she wanted to become a schoolteacher they'd send her to college. But Carole didn't show any interest, and the subject was never raised again.

At her father's suggestion she began to work part-time in the office of a small electronics company he owned. She was very competent, and soon was working full-time, handling orders and some of the bookkeeping. Five years later her father was forced by bad health to sell his business. She stayed on and continued her routine duties. The new owner of the business was a large electronics company, with branch offices in many cities. When the original company was acquired it underwent major changes, and expanded. In the years that followed, Carole saw new people hired and others promoted, but her position didn't change. In spite of her competence and her seven years seniority, she remained an assistant. She'd gotten married, on impulse; later the marriage was annulled and her career began to take on new meaning for her. She dreamed of an executive position at the company's New York or Washington office. She hoped and she waited. She hoped someone would discover what she wanted; she waited for the promotion to be handed to her without her asking for it. She grew more and more dissatisfied. Her dissatisfaction gave way to feeling helpless, to silent despair, and finally hopelessness.

PROBLEM: Carole felt helpless when she found herself in a situation where she had to implement change, when change depended on her speaking up for what she wanted.

Solution

A. Evaluate Self-talk

I asked Carole to listen to the messages she was giving herself about the situation at work. Her underlying irrational statements were:

1. If I'm good and don't make trouble, I'll get what I want.
2. It's all a matter of luck, and who likes you.
3. The best things happen when you don't expect them, or even ask for them.
4. All things come to those who wait.
5. If I'm pretty and charming, someone will do it for me.
6. If they like me, they'll promote me.

Unfortunately, Carole was only daydreaming about getting ahead. She wasn't analyzing the situation at work or planning how to advance. Carole began to substitute rational statements to herself:

1. So-and-so planned her career. So can I.
2. So-and-so asked for her promotion and got it.
3. If I want to get ahead, I'll do it myself.
4. If you want something, you've got to go after it.
5. If I want something, I've got to ask for it. This isn't a popularity contest.
6. If they consider me and my work valuable, they'll promote me.

B. Make an Accomplishment List

Carole also made an accomplishment list. This helped her to become aware of what she was doing for herself. Every day she recorded what she'd done that she liked, and then praised herself for it. She included even small acts that weren't related to her job. Every time she recorded one, she said to herself, "I did that." She gave herself positive messages: "The people who get things done are the ones who do it themselves."

C. Do some Research

At my suggestion, Carole began to make long-range career plans. She asked herself where she wanted to be in a year; and in five years. She gave thought to how she planned to get there; what courses she needed, and what other skills; whom she needed to know. She examined the career paths of several women she admired.

D. Create a Personal Image of the Future

She also used imagery to see herself in the future as an executive woman. She saw herself functioning effectively in her new office. Seeking out projects that would make her visible. She was problem solving in an effective way. She was taking risks and giving orders to her subordinates. She imagined herself in detail, going to board meetings and taking part in conferences. She was dressing more chicly and carrying herself with greater assurance. She had created a new, more satisfying, image of herself, as a woman who made things happen.

E. Learn Assertive Skills

Carole had trouble asking for what she wanted because she'd had little practice at it. I suggested she do some assertive training, and read a book on assertion, such as *When I Say No, I Feel Guilty,* by Manuel Smith. I explained the techniques to her, which are discussed in Chapter Five of this book. She needed to get experience in asking for things and expressing feelings directly. Carole soon became more comfortable with the idea of creating her own career, but she still felt somewhat anxious about asserting herself.

F. Use GPE for Assertiveness

Because she had high anxiety about asserting herself, I suggested she build a GPE hierarchy for assertiveness. Using deep muscle relaxation and a pleasant reinforcing scene, she worked her way up the hierarchy until she was not at all anxious about asserting herself. This was her hierarchy:

SUD	SITUATION
20	Asking a woman she works with to lend her a nail file
30	Asking a newstand man to change a ten dollar bill
40	Telling the boss she has to leave early
50	Asking people in a supermarket line to let her go first because she has only one item
60	Telling a cab driver to close his window
70	Telling a friend she disagrees with him or her about a political candidate
80	Arranging for and going on a job interview for a new position
90	Discussing her job dissatisfaction and career goals with a supervisor
100	Asking for a promotion

After she experienced the hierarchy in imagery and without anxiety, she then worked her way up from the least difficult to the most difficult situations in real life. Each time she took a step, she reinforced herself with praise: "That's done like a very competent person"; "I really handled that well"; "I really know how to take care of myself"; "I really know how to get what I want"; "I'm very competent at handling my environment"; "*I* made that happen"; "I did that myself, and nobody else helped me"; "What a good feeling it is to be in control of your own destiny." Finally Carole was able to ask for a promotion—and got it. When I last saw her, she was very happy in her new job.

IDENTIFYING CLOSELY WITH THE BOSS: JANET

Janet was very close to her boss. He was a public relations director for a big computer firm, and was charismatic and successful. She was hired to be on his staff soon after she finished college. Her main interest on the job quickly became taking care of him. He was high power, and it was exciting working with him. She met important people through him, yet she never used the contacts to further her career, but only for her boss. In a sense, she was like a second wife to him. She identified with his successes but didn't think much about her own.

She traveled with him and was liked by everyone because she was so personable, competent, easy to be with, dependable, and bright. As he moved up in the company he took her along with him. She did all the back-breaking details for him; a lot of the ideas he got credit for came from her. It almost seemed worthwhile when he introduced her as "my right arm." She felt a surge of pride to be associated with such a glamorous figure.

Several years went by; he was near the top. One day he called Janet in and told her that since he'd recently had a promotion he needed a staffer with more academic background, and that he was bringing in a young woman fresh out of graduate school with an M.B.A. He explained to Janet the work was too much for her. It was true she hadn't furthered her education; she'd been so busy devoting her time to him, she never broadened her power base either. She had contacts but they were for him, not for her.

His new assistant was an attractive, competent young woman. She had a different relationship with him than Janet did: She used him as a mentor not as a husband. She made appearances on her own. People asked her to come and consult because he couldn't take all the assignments. She was making contacts and getting projects for herself, with his approval. She was getting visibility, working on committees, sending out notices with her name on them. On some material her name was appearing right under her boss's. He asked her opinion and held conferences with her often, as he did with Janet, but he gave her credit when she worked on a project. Janet clearly was being relegated to a lower position, and she was extremely upset about it.

PROBLEM: Janet had begun to resent her boss and dwell on her unfair treatment. She brooded, thinking, "This is the thanks I get after all I've done for him." She became bitter and developed a negative attitude in the office, and could barely be cordial to the new assistant. A new situation was created where she was the outsider. She became discouraged and gave up trying.

Solution

A. Evaluate Self-talk

I asked Janet, every time a situation arose in which she felt angry or defeated, to tune in to what she said to herself about it, to become aware of negative thoughts and helpless views of the relationships.

1. This is the thanks I get after all I've done for him.
2. He used me, but he's not going to use me any more.
3. Why should I try, they'll just get credit for it.
4. I'm old, why bother trying. I can't make it anyway. She's young.

Janet's negative statements were a self-fulfilling prophecy. She was putting everyone against her. Helplessness leads to depression. She was saying she was helpless, there was nothing she could do about the situation. It was important that she stop seeing herself as a victim and begin to make full use of her assets. Her negative thoughts about the woman assistant were:

5. She's smarter, has better contacts, is prettier and younger, better educated, and has a nicer personality than I.

These were the things she felt helpless about, and thought she couldn't change. We analyzed the situation and her statements about it realistically. She was then able to substitute the following realistic and positive statements about her feelings toward the new assistant:

1. *Information.* She did get more information, but I can organize myself and find out where to get the same or better information, and be as knowledgeable as I choose to be. She doesn't have a monopoly on information. She doesn't have the kind of practical knowledge I have gotten through experience, and which can be gotten only through experience.

2. *Contacts.* Yes, she's made contacts for herself. But I know more people. All I have to do is use the contacts I made through the boss. And use them for myself. That shouldn't be difficult; I've had years of experience with these people. I can learn from her.

3. *Younger.* Yes, she's younger and right now prettier. But there are lots of things I can do to get prettier. I've been neglecting myself. I've become complacent. Maybe this will be good for me. This challenge will make me pay more attention to my appearance.

B. Assess Abilities

What does Janet have? What are her assets? She has the contacts and experience. She has a lot of knowledge about the business. What does she need? Janet decided she could develop some skills. She signed up for a management course, a computer course, and some lessons on public speaking. She also decided she needed to lose ten pounds, so she joined an exercise class. She had a makeup analysis, to learn the modern way of applying makeup, had her hair colored because she was going a little grey, and also got a new hairstyle. She explored some magazines to find out what executive women were wearing, and bought a couple of suits, instead of the form-fitting, frilly dresses she had been wearing.

C. Learn Assertive Skills

Janet attended a workshop on assertiveness. I recommended she read the books on assertion referred to in Chapter Five. We also practiced some of the techniques described in that chapter. Janet needed to learn to assert herself, to take care of her own needs, and to take a more active role in getting what she wanted. She needed to plan some specific strategies, making use of the contacts and inside information she had. For example, one of her contacts liked Japanese gardens. She bought a book on Japanese gardens, called him, mentioned she saw it while browsing in a bookstore, and thought he might like it. This gave her an opportunity to relate to him on a more personal level.

D. Create a Personal Image of the Future

Janet saw herself after she'd lost ten pounds as she had been in another period in her life. She's dressed in clothes out of a businesswoman's magazine; she's wearing heels that are higher than the flat shoes she was wearing. Her hair is shorter, very trim, and brown, instead of salt and pepper. She is lightly made up. She feels much more confident because she knows that she has assertive skills to handle situations that might arise. And she has credits for a year's special training as a computer analyst and in office management. She's more sure of her knowledge, and she can hear herself answering questions with a great deal of assurance.

She saw herself making contacts and telling them it's her

responsibility to take care of the situation, and if there's any problem they can call her. She's assuming authority. She's friendly with her boss, seeing herself acting in an assured, confident manner, expecting and getting respect.

LOW EXPECTATIONS: GAIL

Gail comes from a working-class background where the women did nothing but housework or kept semiskilled factory jobs. It was a struggle for her even to finish high school. She worked afternoons when she was a sophomore. Eventually she had to drop out and finish high school at night. She was bright, but she never thought much of herself. Later, she got a full-time job as a bookkeeper for a chain store. Gail didn't have much ambition or ideas about getting ahead. She was glad to have the position; after all, it was a step up from the kind of work her mother and sisters had done.

Gail's mother is an overweight housewife. Her father would often come home drunk, and on several occasions beat his wife. There are seven children in the family. Gail thought she had it made because she was getting a good salary, while her mother was a household drudge. She was happy she could buy herself nice clothes and take a week's vacation every year. Her job wasn't very interesting, but she could accept being bored with it.

She went along for a long time not realizing things could be any other way. One day she met one of her friends from high school, who was doing very well, working for a company similar to hers. Gail began to wonder about her career. Her friend urged her to join a women's group she belonged to. When Gail joined she saw women from similar backgrounds but who had high expectations of themselves. She was impressed by the ambitious goals they set for themselves. She realized that she too could get more out of life. But how?

PROBLEM: Gail was dissatisfied with what she was doing; she

thought of herself as just one of the girls in the office but didn't know how or where to start making changes. She wanted something else—a different identity.

Solution

A. Use Models

Gail set up some new role models. She subscribed to *Savvy* and other businesswomen's magazines, and got herself into that kind of thinking. She joined a women's group to broaden her social contacts with women who were motivated and goal- and career-oriented. She would watch these women and pick out the traits they had that she liked. She gathered from several women the traits she was most comfortable with, and began incorporating them into her own personality.

B. Assess Abilities

I asked her to make a list of the assets and skills she already had, and to evaluate them. And then study the job market. Where could she fit in with the skills she had? In what areas would her experience and abilities be assets? Did she have strong interests in a field where she lacked appropriate skills?

C. Learn New Skills

After she identified her interest area, Gail decided what she wanted and where she wanted to be. Then she started researching possible job openings, got information by asking people and looking in newspapers, and going to executive recruiters. She found out what other skills she needed. Since she had decided she wanted something in accounting, she signed up for several accounting courses. If you have a problem similar to Gail's, find out what other skills you need, and then inquire where you can get them.

D. Learn Assertive Techniques

Gail also needed some assertiveness training, because she wasn't used to standing up for what she wanted. Assertiveness training would prepare Gail for asking for a promotion within her present company, benefit her on job interviews, and eventually help her handle herself as an executive.

CAN'T ASK FOR A RAISE OR PROMOTION: BOBBIE

Bobbie was a fifty-year-old woman employed as an executive secretary. She had worked for her boss for fifteen years and knew his business inside out. When he was away she ran the office and made many important decisions. She was competent and bright. Over the years her responsibilities had increased greatly. But she was still getting a secretarial salary even though she was functioning in a managerial capacity, and her title was administrative assistant.

PROBLEM: Bobbie was too passive to ask for a raise or a title commensurate with her duties. She had an unrealistic evaluation of herself. She wasn't projecting an executive image.

Solution

A. Assess Abilities

I asked Bobbie to evaluate herself realistically. What executive duties was she already handling? What were her managerial qualifications? If she wanted to advance herself, it would have to be in another department or company. She was so entrenched in the present condition that it would be difficult for her to rise above the role that her boss and co-workers were so used to seeing her in.

In order to reevaluate her personal dress and style I asked her to bring in a recent snapshot of herself and objectively describe what she saw: "I see a middle-aged woman, plain, hair severely pulled back, thin and round-shouldered. Her pants are too big and out of style, her blouse is shabby, her shoes are what my mother would call 'sensible' or 'sturdy.'"

I suggested that she, like Janet, do some research about what new clothes and other changes would be appropriate for her executive image. Bobbie was dowdy. She was still dressing and acting like a secretary. She needed to update her image and get a modern executive look and attitude. I had her buy a couple of well-tailored suits with skirts that concealed the fact that she was underweight. She joined an exercise class to improve her posture. Because she was chronically fatigued, she saw a nutritionist and improved her eating habits.

B. Create a Personal Image of the Future

I asked Bobbie to close her eyes and see herself a few months in the future, with a new physical image of herself. She saw herself with her hair a little fuller, freshly washed, studs in her ears, a string of pearls around her neck under her silk blouse. She had a vital, straight posture; she held her head up. She had on a well-cut suit and pumps to match. Her silk blouse was a soft color, flattering to her face. There was a hint of color in her cheeks, and her eyes were enlarged by a touch of makeup. Her face looked different, and her skin looked fresh from a good base. She was more alert and interested in life. Then she saw herself as an executive, in an executive office, calm and assured, with a gracious manner, dictating to her secretary the agenda of the day.

C. Learn Assertive Skills

To be more outgoing and make social contacts, I recommended that Bobbie, like Gail, acquire some assertive skills. She also joined a women's business association.

D. Learn to Give Orders

Bobbie wasn't used to giving orders. I had her first practice giving orders using imagery, with situations she made up, ranging from easy to difficult. Bobbie didn't need to use GPE because it was not a matter of anxiety getting in her way. She simply needed some experience to help her see herself in the position of one who gives orders.

- Ask someone to deliver a package for her before a certain time.
- Tell the maintenance people to clean her office and be sure to get under her desk.
- Order somebody in the typing pool to do something over again.
- Have someone move her desk to another part of the room where she can get better light.
- Tell the secretary in what sequence she wants her work done.
- Tell the secretary that she wants her to work late tomorrow night.

When she was comfortable giving orders in imagery, we went on to practice in real life. She rehearsed in my office with me, beginning with orders on a small scale and then working up to more important ones. Soon she was comfortable and confident with her new skill, and she could give orders in a firm but friendly way in real life.

E. Learn New Skills

Bobbie's interest in reading was very limited. We scheduled at least thirty minutes a day for her to read and familiarize herself with current national and international events. She improved her conversational skills this way and began to feel more confident and comfortable at business social events.

Gradually, Bobbie changed her image. She had the look of an executive woman, and soon was job hunting. Eventually she found a better position as a manager in another company.

9 SEX IN THE OFFICE

You meet a man socially. If there's an attraction and the conditions are right, it might be appropriate for romance to follow. In business, the rules are different. You meet the same man at the office, and whether you're attracted or not, the rule is: Business and romance don't mix.

Times have changed since the Victorian era. Today people take sex much more casually, and women are freer to direct their own lives. But the double standard of yesteryear is alive and well in the business world. If it becomes known that a woman has had sex with her boss, not only men but other women will lose respect for her. They will attribute whatever success she has to the sexual relationship, no matter how talented or intelligent she is.

Sometimes a man in the office will use his workplace as a hunting ground; he'll be constantly on the make. Other men may use sex to put a woman down, because they aren't comfortable treating a woman as a peer. Another way sexuality might come into play would be through some old, outworn habits of your own. If you're under stress or feeling insecure you might lean on the female ploys and flirtatious daddy's-little-girl tactics that got you what you wanted when you were a child.

Perhaps you, like many women, were raised to believe that your sexual attractiveness is a major part of your identity and value as a human being. From the time you were little, advertising and movie stereotypes have bombarded you with the idea that you need to be alluring and desirable to men. It is often difficult for a woman entering business to drop these habits. You may feel rejected when the men at work treat you like one of the boys.

COQUETTISHNESS OR FLIRTING TO GET HER WAY: LUCY

Lucy is an attractive, blonde, slender young woman who came to me saying that her boss had begun making passes at her. When we analyzed the situation, it turned out that she had been doing very well in her new job, but whenever she wasn't completely sure of herself, when she made a mistake or wanted time off, or didn't want to do something, she smiled and acted coquettish and flirty. The boss started making passes at her because he misinterpreted what she was doing as coming on to him; she was, inadvertently, giving him messages that she was available.

PROBLEM: She was flirting to get her way. Instead of dealing with situations assertively, she was using her sexuality. The boss got the wrong message. He interpreted it as a sexual come-on and responded accordingly.

Solution

A. Examine Belief System
I asked Lucy to make a list of her beliefs about how to get

preferential treatment on the job. She wrote down:

1. If this is how I can get what I want, then this is what I'll do.
2. I'll use what I have to get what I want.
3. If I'm cute, they'll give me extras.

Since these beliefs had led to inappropriate behaviors and negative consequences, I asked her to challenge them and substitute alternative beliefs that would lead to appropriate behaviors and productive consequences.

NEGATIVE	POSITIVE
1. If this how I can get what I want, then this is what I'll do.	1. I may get what I want, but I'm paying a high price in my self-esteem, and other people's esteem. I can get what I want by merit. I'm intelligent enough to get what I want. I don't have to flirt for it.
2. I'll use what I have to get what I want.	2. I can get what I want by using other things I have—and like myself better.
3. If I'm cute, they'll give me extras.	3. But they won't respect me. And I want respect.

B. Use a Model

I recommended that Lucy choose a role model, a woman who was successful, whom she respected and admired. I asked her to observe the way she acted around men at the office, to notice how she handled situations differently from the way Lucy did, and to experiment adapting some of her model's tactics to her own style.

C. Assess Appearance

If you have a problem similar to Lucy's, I suggest you try something else I asked her to do: Look in the mirror. Check your clothes when you're ready for work. Are they tightly fitted? Revealing? Do you wear frills? Very high heels? Too much perfume or jewelry? A seductive hairstyle? Heavy makeup? Your look should be smart, relaxed, and natural.

D. Use GPE for Not Getting Special Treatment

Lucy still felt quite a bit of anxiety when men did not treat her as a sexually attractive, feminine person. When her co-workers treated her like one of the boys, and didn't give her extra goodies for being a woman—easier assignments, the best hours, the pleasantest desk—she got upset. We built the following hierachy for her:

SUD	SITUATION
30	A man doesn't open the door for her or pull out her chair
40	On a bus a man lets her stand and takes a seat
50	She has to carry a movie projector or a very heavy attaché case and no one helps her with it; everyone stands and watches
60	Men make a dirty joke in her presence
80	She has her hair cut and no one notices it
90	She's sitting at a table with some men as a beautiful woman walks by, and they make comments about how attractive the woman is, as if she isn't there

After several GPE sessions, it wasn't long before Lucy was feeling little or no anxiety in these situations when they occurred in her daily life.

E. Learn Assertive Skills

Lucy learned some assertive responses so she could ask for

what she wanted in a positive, friendly, assertive manner. She also needed practice saying no. If you feel that you have a similar problem, the techniques in Chapter Five will also help you develop these skills.

Eventually Lucy was very comfortable with a direct, businesslike, womanly manner. She found that the men she worked with treated her with greater respect and were more receptive to her requests and opinions. I suggested that she keep in mind the following pointers in her interactions with her boss.

1. Analyze what you want from the boss and from the situation. If you're giving a presentation, make it very clear. Be very well prepared. The secret is to be well prepared so you don't have to lean on anything else.

2. Practice behavior in imagery. See yourself talking to the boss. Be very clear in your mind what you want. Ask specific questions. See yourself taking time and giving very thoughtful answers.

3. Speak slowly. Listen. Analyze what you want and what he wants. Say to yourself: "The best way to handle this is to be logical and and calmly convincing. A man leans on persuasion, rationale."

Lucy reported to me later that their relationship had returned to a firm, businesslike footing, and the issue of sex did not come up again.

Many forms of sexual harassment occur on the job today, ranging from a familiar pat on the shoulder to a boss's demand that you sleep with him. Sometimes a co-worker will make off-color remarks, or undress you with his eyes while you speak to him. The fact that you are less powerful in certain situations may cause others to try to take advantage of their authority.

Some men in business constantly test women, not even expecting results. Remember, a man won't be devastated if you turn him down. He'll think, "You can't win 'em all." But be aware that a fragile male ego is under all that bravado, so it's important to leave his self-esteem intact. I'm sure you're aware that men and woman approach sex with different attitudes. Often a woman approaches sex with romantic notions of love and commitment. A man, particularly in business, usually does not, so it's important for you to keep work situations completely professional. No matter how attracted you are to a colleague, client, or customer, keep the relationship strictly business. A sexual involvement could cost you your job.

DEALING WITH CHAUVINISM: ROZ

Roz was working late one evening when her immediate supervisor came into her office, put his arm around her shoulder and said, "Say, I have an idea. Why don't we go up to my place? I could fix us a snack, and we could finish this work up there."

PROBLEM: How to handle a colleague who is testing her to see if she's sexually available.

Solution

A. Assess the Situation

Basically, Roz needed to analyze the situation. She didn't have a clear idea of what she expected from the men she worked with or from herself. She was afraid of hurting their feelings, and they were quick to sense this. She needed to make up her mind just what she would accept and what she would not accept from them.

B. Practice Businesslike Behavior in Imagery

I suggested that she create an image of herself dealing with her male colleagues in a business situation. She saw herself in conversations with them while on a business trip, during and after a meeting. I had her imagine herself speaking in a friendly businesslike way. She is dressed in a smart, good-looking suit. At the meeting she is well prepared. She knows what she wants to accomplish, is organized, and sticks to the business at hand. She appears confident and efficient. Her manner is formal though casual. During a coffee break she talks in a relaxed but impersonal way with some of the men. As the meeting breaks up one of the men asks her out for a drink, and she says, "No, thanks, I have to finish the report."

I asked Roz to imagine this and similar scenes in detail so she could see herself relating to male colleagues in a comfortable, relaxed, businesslike way. With repeated practice in imagery, Roz was, over a period of time, able to strengthen her self-image as an assertive, clear-minded executive woman.

Strategies for Handling Male-Female Situations in the Office

A well-known lawyer once told me that he had noticed the three women lawyers in his office each had a different sexual style. The first was always trying to be like a man. She came on like gangbusters, and was always trying to top him. The second was experienced, cooperative and professional. She was efficient, and knew where she was in her business relationships. She didn't try to compete with him. He got along best with her. The third woman was competent, but when she wasn't sure of herself she'd use her femininity, her charm, to convince him. She'd give a little sexual dimension to their conversation. Interestingly enough, the one he confessed to testing the most, sexually, was the aggressive one. Her pushiness made him want to put her down, and he was least cooperative with her because he felt so antagonized.

If you see a woman wearing spike heels and a lot of perfume and lace, you aren't going to take her too seriously, and neither are the men she works with. In the office, you can be womanly without being "feminine" and frilly. Like Roz, you can create an image of yourself as a womanly, competent person, who keeps her business and personal life separate. You can learn to turn your sexuality off and on when you want. You will realize you can be a sexual woman when you choose to be, at an appropriate time, when it's beneficial to you. You don't have to respond to someone else's stimulus or demands.

On the job you can avoid potential come-ons. In these cases an ounce of prevention is worth a pound of cure.

1. Don't wear sexy clothes.
2. Don't fish for compliments about your appearance from the men at work.
3. Avoid discussing your personal life with any male colleague.
4. Don't ask for personal favors or special treatment or favors that aren't related to work, from a male boss or manager.
5. Soon after you enter a department, find out who the possible troublemakers are, and avoid these men.
6. Make sure it gets around that you're involved; mention your husband's or boyfriend's name.
7. Don't let anyone get away with an obvious pass. Don't pretend it didn't happen.

Learn to recognize the early signs of a male come-on. If a man at the office seems to be getting too chummy lately, ask yourself the following questions.

1. Are his conversations with me more about personal matters and less about business?
2. Does he discuss his sex life, love life, or family problems with me?

3. Does he ask intimate questions about my sex, love, or family life?
4. Does he make frequent physical contact—touching my arm or shoulder, or brushing against me accidentally?
5. Does he often compliment my looks? Say how attractively I'm dressed?
6. Does he tell me dirty jokes?

If you've answered yes to several of these, it's wise to look out; you may be in for trouble.

If a man at work does make a pass at you, your first instinct may be to panic or to pretend it isn't happening or that it's funny and giggle at it. These are the worst reactions you could make. You must treat the situation seriously. You can say something like, "I thought our relationship was on a different basis," or "I think you misunderstand our relationship, and my feelings toward you." You can blame it on yourself: "I hope I haven't given you the wrong idea about things."

CRITICISM AND REJECTION

10

"You did this all wrong!" How do you feel when someone says that to you? Is it hard to take? To a lot of women it is. If you're uncomfortable with criticism, you may be seeing it as a personal attack, a comment on you. You must be able to see criticism as directed not at you, but at the task or work you've done. If you can make the separation, then you can see the situation as something you have control over and can correct. It's important to realize that you're not being evaluated as a human being.

Girls don't learn, as boys do, that criticism helps improve their playing ability. The result is that women do not use criticism for growth. Their response to criticism is to give up, to think "I'm no good," and to make negative statements to others about themselves. But a man asks himself: "What can I learn from this?" How wise the person was who said, "I learn more from my enemies than from my friends." Few women think of this bit of wisdom when they're being criticized.

Rejection is also difficult for women because they have

been taught to pay attention to the quality of relationships. A woman's whole existence has been attuned to them—father, mother, boyfriends—her identity has been enmeshed in her relationships. Rejection is serious to a woman because she feels her identity is on the line. She's concerned with whether people like and approve of her. As a result she makes acceptance terribly important.

But a man is judged more by the job he does. He develops ways of acting that help him get what he wants. He wants respect rather than to be liked or loved. A woman gives the people in her life a lot of power. She's been taught to please, so she pleases across the board, and thinks: "Everybody should love me." For many women, life is a popularity contest.

NEEDING EVERYONE TO LOVE HER: NANCY

Nancy, twenty-eight, is blond, attractive, and vivacious. She is outgoing and thrives on people and people's attentiveness. Her friends describe her as "sweet" because she is so accommodating and easy to please. When she was young, all she had to do was smile, and people made a fuss over her. Her parents were proud of her and liked to show her off. She was very popular in high school and a teacher's pet. In fact, she was everyone's darling, and grew up expecting, in her naive way, that that's the way life would be. When she got a business degree from a local college, her family made a big fuss over her. She got her first job through her father's influence. He was vice-president of a large chemical company, and one of his golf partners placed Nancy in a job as management trainee for a rubber company that was a subsidiary.

When she started working she felt uncomfortable with the impersonal business atmosphere. She realized she had a job to do and she was expected to do it. The head of her department would tell her to research data and prepare reports. He'd give her instructions impersonally and then dismiss her. She felt he wasn't interested in her at all because he seemed so cold and displeased. She wondered what she was doing to make him act that way. On the job she didn't get much positive feedback. Most of the time when people told her to do things they addressed her in a perfunctory businesslike way; she started losing her self-confidence and feeling rejected.

PROBLEM: Nancy had never experienced anyone who ignored her charm. To her it meant rejection.

Solution

A. Examine Belief System

Nancy had to make the distinction between the business world and home and school life. In home life you can expect one thing, in real life you expect something else. She needed a realistic view of the business world. In the business world you don't get patted on the head for every brilliant remark. She needed to change her expectations and decide what her goals and purposes are. She's not working to win popularity contests and admiration and approval, but to get her job done well.

B. Evaluate Self-talk

I asked Nancy to make a list of the messages she was giving herself about the situation with her boss. She decided these were:

1. He doesn't appreciate me.
2. He doesn't approve of me.
3. He doesn't like me.
4. He never compliments me.

Then she challenged these messages with positive realistic statements.

NEGATIVE	POSITIVE
1. He doesn't appreciate me.	1. If he didn't think my work was competent I wouldn't be working here.
2. He doesn't approve of me.	2. He's being businesslike and expects me to be the same.
3. He doesn't like me.	3. Being patted on the head feels good to a child but it's patronizing to an adult. He's treating me like an adult and peer.
4. He never compliments me.	4. Rewards in business come in different ways. He takes it for granted I'm a professional and do good work.

Each time she found herself having a negative thought about herself and her boss, she made herself switch to one of the positive statements.

C. Use Thought-stopping

Because Nancy was dwelling on negative thoughts she used thought-stopping. When she thought: "The boss doesn't like me or approve of me," she told herself to Stop! Switch! and used a positive statement, like "I have no proof of that"; "It's just not his style to comment or praise"; or "I wouldn't be here if he didn't approve of my work." After a while she didn't have to say "Stop! Switch!" She simply replaced the negative thought with the positive. Eventually the negative ones were occurring less and less frequently.

D. Use a Model

I asked Nancy to observe a woman executive whose appearance was businesslike and who was self-motivated, self-sufficient, and not dependent on the approval of others.

E. Practice Behavior in Imagery

She visualized herself as a motivated, self-sufficient businesswoman in work situations. She imagined experiencing the good feelings that come from an *inner* satisfaction of accomplishing things, her self-worth increasing and being fed by *her* own evaluation of her work.

Several months later Nancy reported that she was feeling more comfortable with her boss and his impersonal style. Her attitude toward her job became more positive, and she had received a memo telling her she was in line for a promotion.

TAKING CRITICISM PERSONALLY: LUCILLE

Lucille was recently hired as an assistant manager in the personnel department of a large shipping company, and was very eager to do a good job. One morning she gave a report in a meeting, which her boss, the personnel director, criticized harshly in front of her colleagues. He said curtly, "That type of report isn't going to do us any good. You don't have nearly enough data for us to base our new promotion strategy on. Reynolds, let's hear what you have for us." Later that day he came up to her in a very friendly way and chatted about whether she was happy with the travel arrangements for a trip she was about to take. Lucille was confused. He talked to her as if nothing unpleasant had happened, although she felt personally attcked by his comments in the meeting.

From then on, every time he criticized her work, she would get discouraged. She found herself making more and more mistakes, becoming unsure of herself, and feeling incompetent. She noticed that when the men she worked with were criticized they didn't let it get to them the same way. Soon she began to have serious doubts about her ability.

PROBLEM: Lucille took criticism as a negative evaluation of

herself. She thought that since she made one mistake she was worthless. To her, criticism of her work meant rejection of her as a person. She forgot all her successes, all her assets and strong points.

Solution

A. Evaluate Self-talk

I suggested Lucille examine the statements she was making to herself when she was criticized:

1. I can't do anything right. I do everything wrong.
2. The boss will see I'm incompetent and fire me.
3. My colleagues will look down on me and not take me seriously.
4. I don't know as much as I should know. I don't belong here.
5. The boss is annoyed with me. I'll never be able to please him.

After she listed them it became apparent to her that they were irrational and were distorting her view of being criticized. She saw how these thoughts were responsible for many of the negative feelings she was having about herself and the job. She developed a rational response to each statement:

IRRATIONAL	RATIONAL
1. I can't do anything right. I do everything wrong.	1. That's not accurate. There are many things I do right. Sometimes, because I'm human, I may do something wrong. All my other reports were satisfactory.
2. The boss will see I'm incompetent and fire me.	2. I'm not incompetent. There are people who've been on the job longer

3. My colleagues will look down on me and not take me seriously.

4. I don't know as much as I should know. I don't belong here.

5. The boss is annoyed with me. I'll never be able to please him.

than I have and are not working up to my standards.

3. He's criticized a lot of competent people and others respect them. There's no reason why they won't respect me.

4. This may be true about a specific aspect of my job. Here's something I've got to work on. I need more work in this area. He's right; I'm glad he told me, that's the way I'll learn. I'm glad he's the kind of boss who let's you know and doesn't hold everything in. It gives you a chance to learn.

5. Yes, he's annoyed with me for the moment, but he can't always be happy. On the whole my work is satisfactory.

B. Use GPE for Criticism
Because Lucille had high anxiety about being criticized, she built a GPE hierarchy for criticism:

SUD	SITUATION
25	Someone tells her she looked better in the dress she had on when she was thinner
30	She says the wrong thing at a meeting and someone reminds her of it afterward
45	Her boss gives her back a report and tells her it

could have been done much better and needs more work

70   Her boss, during her annual performance appraisal, says she hasn't met her goals for the year

75   A superior complains to her boss in front of her that she's inefficient and doesn't know her business

90   She's singled out at a board meeting for substandard performance

Lucille copied each scene onto an index card and arranged them with the lowest SUD-rated scene on top. She began practicing relaxation exercises at home, and after two sessions was ready to expose herself to the criticism hierarchy. Then she read the first card to herself, closed her eyes and imagined herself in the scene for about eight seconds. After erasing the image from her mind she noticed whether her anxiety level had gone up. When it did, she returned to relaxing and imagining pleasant scenes until she was calm again. Then she repeated the first scene. When she succeeded in imagining it with little or no increase in SUD level, she went on to the next card.

Lucille completed all items on the hierarchy without anxiety after seven thirty-minute sessions at home. She noticed she was bothered much less than before by negative feedback at work. Her self-confidence returned and she was once again functioning competently and enjoying her work.

THE BOSS WHO GAVE NO POSITIVE FEEDBACK: CLAIRE

Claire had been on a new job for six months. She didn't know if she was going to be kept on by the company or not, and the uncertainty kept her highly anxious much of the time.

She felt she did her work well, understood the job and what she was doing, but the boss never gave her any positive feedback on her performance. She didn't know whether or not he liked her work, and wondered if she should look for something else. In her previous job, every time she did something well—wrote a good memo or drafted a good report—the boss would acknowledge it with a comment. But not this boss. He had a different managerial style. She had no idea where she stood with him.

PROBLEM: Claire interpreted the absence of feedback as criticism or rejection. When she gave the boss a piece of work she thought was particularly good, she expected him to say something positive about it, but he said nothing. Sometimes he'd ask her to do things again, but he didn't criticize her. When Claire got no feedback, she imagined nothing she did pleased him.

Solution

A. Evaluate Self-Talk

Claire wrote down the irrational statements she was making to herself and disputed each one with a rational response:

IRRATIONAL	RATIONAL
1. He never gives me any feedback. He must be displeased with my work.	1. That's just his style, not to give feedback. I should be able to evaluate my own work. I'll have to evaluate my own work.
2. If he really liked me he'd tell me about it.	2. Why should he tell me when he doesn't tell anyone else?
3. He's probably keeping me temporarily until he finds someone else.	3. I have no proof that he's dissatisfied or that he's looking for someone else.

I've always kept my jobs and done satisfactory work for everyone else and I think I'm doing my usual good work.

B. Learn Reinforcement

Then Claire learned to reinforce herself. When the boss failed to give her reinforcement for doing something, she gave *herself* positive feedback for doing a good job. This generated more self-confidence. First she had to make sure she was really proficient and knew the job and skills. Then she set herself up as a judge of what was a good performance. She commented to herself on the positive aspects of her work. When she gave the boss a report she knew was good, she placed it on his desk in front of him, smiled, and left without expecting any feedback. She made positive statements to herself: "This is a complete report. This is an accurate report." She soon developed more confidence in her own evaluation and no longer looked to the boss to judge her work.

HUSBAND WON'T LIKE HER IF SHE SUCCEEDS: MARY

Mary, thirty-five, felt her husband would resent her if she went up for a job promotion. She was afraid he'd feel threatened if she had more status or was making more money than he. They had a group of friends who were in lower management. They would frequently see these people in the city, and usually took a summer house with them. She was afraid if she took the promotion she'd also lose her friends. And yet she was bored to death in her job. She was brighter and more ambitious than most of her circle, and was more interested in the world than they were. But now that she had the opportunity to lead a more challenging life, she was torn.

Mary came from a lower-middle-class family that lived in a low-income suburban community. The pressure to conform by getting married and having a circle of friends was strong. She married a boy she met at the local community college, and they moved into a modest home in the same neighborhood she had been brought up in. They both had had the same friends ever since high school. She was fond of her friends, and even though they were no longer interested in the same things, the thought of losing them upset her.

The hotel chain she worked for wanted to send her into a training program for middle management. When the chain bought some new hotels the boss recommended they train her because he saw she had executive potential. Since she had a daughter, fifteen, who was pretty much on her own, Mary saw nothing at home to stand in the way of taking the position she was offered. The job meant a chance to travel. But her great fear was that she would lose her husband. She was afraid that having a better position than his would hurt the marriage and lower his estimation of himself. Also, she was comfortable with her old group of friends, doing pretty much the same things they'd being doing since high school. She wasn't sure what life would be like without them.

PROBLEM: Mary feared that personal success might destroy her marriage and alter a comfortable, though dull, lifestyle.

Solution

A. Evaluate the Situation
Mary had to face the reality that if she became a successful executive, it might threaten her marriage. Was she willing to take that risk? There are things she could do that would help the marriage survive the transition period. The first step

would be to establish good communication with her husband, discussing the move with him so he feels he's in on the decision-making process. She should give him the respect of consulting him on the matter. If he has very strong feelings against it she knows it's a definite threat to the marriage. She has to make a decision at that point whether the marriage is important to her. I recommended that she talk to her husband in a caring, reassuring manner: "I can imagine if I were you how I'd be feeling resentful and put down. But I rely on you for emotional support and warmth, and the most important values in my life. My relationship with you is still the most important thing to me." In this way she lets him know that her success does not mean she needs him less or that he and the marriage are now less important to her. He may feel threatened by her increased financial independence. She must tell him she depends on him for love and the primary relationship in her life.

If he agrees it's a good idea that she take the job, she should never let him forget how important he is to her. She should help build his self-esteem, and perhaps guide him into a better job so they can build their lives together. She should get him to find things they can do outside the group, explore new possibilities for intimacy with their family, so that their main source of amusement doesn't go out with the old friends. When he becomes more assured and confident, then she can bring him into her new social life with the friends she's made in business. As for the old friends, there are always some who are closer than others, and if the relationship is based on more than just a habit, then the friendships can be continued. She should analyze which relationships she's outgrown and which she wants to continue.

B. Learn Assertive Skills

Mary needed assertiveness training to make it easier for her to say no to old friends when they insisted she come back and join them in activities that no longer interested her.

C. Create a Personal Image of the Future

Mary created an image of her life as it would be after taking the new position. She pictured herself interested and stimulated by the new challenges, and learning and acquiring new skills. She saw herself and her husband now enjoying new experiences, exploring new interests together. They have grown closer as a result of her increased moral support and interest in his life and career. They've made new friends through their new activities, and maintained some of the old friendships with people they genuinely felt close to.

She practiced creating these images at least once a day until she became comfortable with her new self-image.

MAKING UNPOPULAR CHANGES: LISA

Lisa made a procedure change in the office where she was assistant division manager, and was criticized for it by others in the office. She had calculated the risk involved and decided it was a good one. Although she thought it would be a desirable change, the people in the office, who were accustomed to the old way of doing things, strongly objected. They called her a hotshot and accused her of upsetting the apple cart. Lisa had gone to business school and was up on new management techniques. She'd also been in her department a while, so she was very familiar with office procedures. The change she had made wasn't that inconvenient and would eventually mean less work for the employees, once they adjusted to it. Still they grumbled over it.

The criticism and grumbling got to Lisa. She started to doubt her decision and have fears her ideas wouldn't work. She felt extremely uncomfortable among her subordinates, knowing they were annoyed with her, and sensing their hostility. She was convinced that "everyone" disliked her. She began thinking about going back to the old procedure just to please everyone and have them like her again.

PROBLEM: Personal criticism was forcing Lisa to back down on her executive decisions and was making her fearful of taking more initiative in making changes.

Solution

A. Evaluate Self-talk

Lisa was making negative and irrational statements to herself that were having an adverse effect on how she viewed her position:

1. They'll continue to be resistant and hostile, and not cooperate with me.
2. No one will like me anymore.
3. It's going to be disruptive. They'll lose work time. It will be a disaster.
4. Maybe it won't work and I'll be criticized even more. I'll be a failure.

She rethought these statements and dealt with them in a rational way:

IRRATIONAL	RATIONAL
1. They'll continue to be resistant and hostile, and not cooperate with me.	1. Once they see that it's working more smoothly, for their own benefit, they'll be more cooperative.
2. No one will like me anymore.	2. I've got to decide whether I'm going to be manager or run in a popularity contest. This isn't a popularity contest. Everybody doesn't have to love me.

3. It's going to be very disruptive. They'll lose work time. It will be a disaster.

3. It may lose work time now, but I believe they'll make it up later because it'll be more efficient.

4. Maybe it won't work and I'll be criticized even more. I'll be a failure.

4. That may be true, but then I may gain more by being innovative. I calculated the risk, and it's worth the gamble.

B. Learn Assertive Skills

Lisa then learned some assertive responses so she could handle individuals who confronted her with complaints or criticism: "I can understand you wouldn't be comfortable with this. It is different from the old procedure. But I believe it's a more efficient procedure."

C. Use GPE Hierarchy for Criticism Based on Decisions and Judgment

In Lisa's hierarchy, she imagined the following situations:

SUD	SITUATION
30	Ordering stationery for the office and people saying they like the old kind better
40	Painting her apartment and her boyfriend saying he doesn't like the color
50	Switching two secretaries' offices and they complain about it
60	Changing the lunch schedule and getting flak for it
70	Getting a haircut that her friends don't seem to like
80	Making minor changes in office procedure and a subordinate saying he doesn't like it
90	Making an extensive change in office procedure, involving a lot of people, and they complain about it

D. Practice Behavior in Imagery

I had Lisa create an image of herself as a manager. She closed her eyes and saw herself: how she looked, how she was acting when she told people about changes she was making. She had her strategy all planned in her mind. She imagined herself calling a three o'clock meeting and saw herself standing at the head of the table in the board room, dressed appropriately, appearing confident. She noticed what people were there, how her voice would sound, her speech firm yet friendly. In a matter-of-fact professional tone, she announced the changes. She saw herself explaining the changes to the other managers in an authoritative, confident manner.

Before long she was able to accept criticism from her subordinates without feeling intimidated or rejected.

THEY'LL HATE ME IF I SUCCEED: MARCIE

Marcie was an intelligent twenty-eight-year-old who lived at home with her parents and younger sister. Hers was a working-class home where a woman was expected to work until she got married, and quit as soon as the children started arriving. The only unusual training Marcie had was in junior high school, when her school opened up a shop course to girls; she'd joined the class, and found she enjoyed putting things together. She'd become familiar with electrical products. In a basic way, she'd researched electronics. Curiosity led her to build simple electronic gadgets at home. When a job at an electronics firm opened up she siezed the opportunity to work there, hoping to use her knowledge. She started her career as a secretary for the electronics company. In five years she received three salary increases, but remained a secretary to one of the vice-presidents. She was well paid, and enjoyed the camaraderie, the feeling of a girls' club that she shared with the other secretaries. Her family and friends thought her job was excellent, and that she'd done well for a woman.

But after five years there as a secretary, she felt deeply dissatisfied. She wasn't using her skills in electronics or satisfying her interests. The only positive things about the job were the group of friends she had grown close to there and the job security. When she complained to her parents they told her how lucky she was to be getting such a good salary, and to be satisfied with what she had. They discouraged her when she spoke of a career. "You'll be married soon enough," they'd say.

Then, one day, despite her parents' advice and her concerns over distancing herself from her friends, she applied for a managerial position. Her application was considered and she was given the job. But she rejected the offer and came to me confused and upset. She knew she was organized, intelligent, and knowledgeable about electronics, but the idea of changing her status to manager caused her a great deal of anxiety.

PROBLEM: Marcie was afraid her family would disapprove of her and she'd become alienated from them. She was reluctant to give up the security of a familiar, comfortable position for a new job that might not work out. She feared that if she became a manager she'd no longer fit in with her old friends, who might now view her as an outsider.

Solution

Evaluate Self-talk

When I asked her to evaluate her self-talk, Marcie found she was giving herself the following messages:

1. I'll become a stranger to my family.
2. I'll get fired from the new job and not have anything.
3. My friends will think I'm a snob.

4. My father will be disappointed because he'll think I don't want to settle down and have children. My father disapproves of career women.
5. I don't know enough, so I won't do well. They'll find out that I don't fit the job.

She decided that although statements 3 and 4 were rational she was interpreting them negatively. She clarified them in a positive way to herself.

RATIONAL	POSITIVE
3. My friends will think I'm a snob.	3. It's true I'm pretty bored with some of my friends anyway. The ones who are really close I can keep, and it would be nice to meet some interesting new people.
4. My father will be disappointed because he'll think I don't want to settle down and have children. My father disapproves of career women.	4. I love my father, but I have to choose whether I live my life by his values or my needs. He'll get used to it.

Marcie also decided that statements 1, 2, and 5 were irrational messages. She challenged them with rational ones:

IRRATIONAL	RATIONAL
1. I'll become a stranger to my family.	1. This doesn't have to be true. I'll act just the same to them, and they'll adjust to my new position. I can be just as close to them now as before.
2. I'll get fired from my new	2. I wouldn't have gotten the

| job and not have any-thing. | job if I didn't have poten-tial. |
| 5. I don't know enough, so I won't do well. They'll find out that I don't fit the job. | 5. What I don't know I can learn. No one knows the whole job when they take it. If I was proficient enough for them to take me, I'll be proficient enough for them to keep me. I can adapt to the new work. |

B. Assess Abilities

Marcie examined her skills to see if they were adequate. Then she projected for herself a plan of what skills she needed to get where she wanted to be. She took some courses to increase her knowledge of electronics and job-related subjects. She also took a bookkeeping course.

C. Create a Personal Image of the Future

Marcie created an image of herself functioning in the new job. She saw the job in detail. She saw herself getting respect from people, building a support system among her subordinates. People were loyal to her because she treated them with respect and consideration. They're building a fine unit and a feeling of pride in the unit. She imagined herself making decisions and liking it. She created a new self-image, saw herself handling new responsibilities.

D. Practice Behavior in Imagery

She also used imagery to see herself making new friends with women who are her professional peers. She imagined herself talking to them competently about subjects that interested them. When she was comfortable with these images, and after taking the new position, Marcie tried out the behavior in real life. She engaged in actual conversations with women managers at work and gradually came to accept herself as one of them.

E. Learn Assertive Skills

To replace her previous support system, I suggested Marcie join an executive women's organization made up of upwardly oriented women like herself. She soon found a new identity and validation among this group of successful women.

REJECTED FOR BEING A WOMAN: SHEILAH

Sheilah had no trouble in her job as a supervisor in the credit department of a manufacturing company. Then she got a new position in a very conservative firm, in a middle-management training group. She was the first woman to be trained in this group, and one of the first woman managers in the company. It wasn't long before she noticed that in subtle and not-so-subtle ways she was being ignored. When the men went out to lunch they didn't ask her to join them. They passed information around her and "forgot" to tell her about meetings. Even the supporting staff seemed to reject her for being a woman. If she asked for something, the secretaries or clerical workers weren't as cooperative as they were with the men, or sometimes they would do the work she asked for sloppily.

PROBLEM: The men were excluding Sheilah and treating her like a second-rate person. She didn't know how to act when the men snubbed her.

Solution

A. Learn Assertive Skills

Sheilah's main problem was difficulty in asserting herself

and maintaining a credible image as a manager in a situation where attitudes were sexist. I suggested she join an assertiveness training workshop for women being given at the local "Y." In my office we role played the strategies described in Chapter Five.

In addition, I recommended Sheilah try these brief strategies: When she was left out of a meeting, she was to attend the next one and firmly request that everything that had been mentioned in the previous meeting be gone over. I reminded her that the important thing in these situations is not to overreact, but to be firm.

Within two months, Sheilah's new assertive skills and renewed self-confidence were gaining her respect from people who before had slighted her. She was acting with greater competence and self-assurance, and her male co-workers ultimately accepted her as a peer.

B. Strategies If You Think You're Being Ignored

If, like Sheilah, you find information is being passed around you, you may find it useful to make allies of some of the secretaries of peers. If you are on friendly terms with them they can keep you informed of goings-on in the department.

Uncooperative subordinates can be a problem. Giving orders to subordinates who seem disrespectful can be disconcerting. But don't be intimidated. Stick to your guns. Act as if you expect them to do what you request. Be very firm in your request. Don't budge until they do what you ask. Be specific: "I want this done by tomorrow at noon."

Practice the assertive skills you learn by rehearsing them with a friend if you wish. Give orders. When people double-talk you, persist until you can pin them down to an acceptable answer. Remember, you can't have the whole world love you. Respect is the key word.

AUTHORITY FIGURES

11

When you're brought up with the feeling you can't protect yourself, people in authority assume bigger-than-life proportions, because they have the power to hurt or help. Men tend to have a somewhat competitive attitude toward authority figures. Women often see themselves as helpless and powerless in the face of authority. Studies have shown that girls obey the demands of authority figures more than boys do.* Boys are more rebellious and are involved in struggling for dominance among themselves.

Girls tend to fear authority more because they have no sense of their own ability to cope, of being effective in the world. A man will change a tire; a woman stands waiting for help. She feels totally dependent on the good will of other people. She's looking for someone to protect her. She's taught she's fragile and helpless: "You'll get hurt", "You're vulnera-

---

*Eleanor E. Maccoby and Carol Nagy Jacklin, *The Psychology of Sex Differences*, (Stanford University Press, 1974), p. 172.

ble." So she's continually looking for someone to make it safe for her, to protect her.

If this is true of you, then you are constantly at the mercy of others. You try to please them. Because you're not as physically strong as a man, your fragility is encouraged: "Isn't she dainty!" In the business world it's helpful for a woman to be at ease with people in authority. She may need to get a sponsor or mentor, someone in a powerful position who will further her career and stand up for her. She should be able to deal with authority figures in a relaxed, realistic way.

FEAR OF AUTHORITY: LEE

Lee was the middle child in a large family, with three older brothers and three younger sisters. She had a very domineering father, who was strict with his children and could be very unpleasant when he was angry. He had strong ideas of how things should be done. He demanded perfection. Every time her father said something, Lee responded immediately. He took pride in having what he called "push-button children." Her brothers and sisters were all respectful and obedient.

After Lee finished high school she got a job in the office of an insulation projects manufacturing company. She soon became so competent that they transferred her from the office in New Jersey to the main office in New York, where she had a low managerial position. She was cheerful, respectful, and very willing. She was happy in her job because the man she was working for was easygoing, accepting, and pleasant. But when a promotion came up to another department, where the boss was more businesslike and impersonal, Lee hesitated to take it. It was an excellent opportunity, one that would lead to a higher position, but he was the kind of person who made her very anxious. Her experience and training were more than adequate for the new job. What was shaking her confidence were her thoughts and fantasies about dealing with her new boss: He was a big, stern-looking man whom she'd never really spoken to, aside from an occasional "good morning" in the elevator. He often frowned and seemed harsh and humorless. Once she overheard him speaking angrily on the telephone. She was afraid she'd never be able to work comfortably with him because she'd be too nervous. She was thinking of turning the position down.

PROBLEM: Lee viewed her prospective boss as someone she would not be happy working for because she was afraid she couldn't please him. She couldn't work for anyone who seemed the least bit rejecting. Lee had built up an intimidating image of a man she didn't really know, and was reacting to that image. She was frightening herself by imagining and anticipating situations in which she wouldn't be able to function.

Solution

A. Evaluate Self-talk
Lee first made a list of all the messages she was giving herself about the situation.

1. I'll never be able to please him.
2. All he'll do is holler at me and find fault with what I do. He won't approve of anything I do.
3. I won't enjoy working with him.
4. I'll never know when anything is right, if he's always going to be like that.
5. He's a horrible, cold man.

Then she sorted out the irrational statements and challenged them with rational ones:

IRRATIONAL	RATIONAL
1. I'll never be able to please him.	1. I can do the best I can do.

2. All he'll do is holler at me and find fault with what I do. He won't approve of anything I do.
4. I'll never know when anything is right if he's always going to be like that.
5. He's a horrible, cold man.

2. He has an aggressive manner. That's his style. It doesn't necessarily mean he's disapproving.
4. I'll do the best I can.

5. He has a problem showing warmth.

She decided the realistic message was statement 3, and countered its negative tone with a positive one:

NEGATIVE
3. I won't enjoy working with him.

POSITIVE
3. I may not enjoy working with him as much as I might with someone else, but I can't measure everything in terms of enjoyment. I may learn *more* from him than from another boss.

B. Use Thought-stopping

Because Lee kept worrying about the situation, I had her use thought-stopping to put an end to her fantasies of disaster. Every time she began to imagine she was in a situation where she was having trouble with her new boss, she told herself, "Stop! Switch!" and switched to a pleasant reinforcing scene.

C. Humanize the Boss

Lee was blowing authority figures up to beyond their real size. She needed to bring them down to size, to humanize them. I had her tell me about her boss's life, as much as she knew about him through conversations with a mutual acquaintance. She knew he was a tennis player and she, also, played tennis. To have her perceive him differently, I asked her to imagine seeing him on the tennis court. She pictured herself very relaxed, trim, confident, because she knew she played a good game of tennis. She was waiting for her boss and another man to finish playing. The boss was having a bad game. He was clumsy, and his hair was mussed. When he missed the ball he'd make jokes to hide his embarrassment. As he walked off the court he seemed visibly upset, and when he saw Lee he became flustered and dropped his racket and tried to smooth back his hair. Then, with a sheepish laugh shrugged his shoulders and said, "You can't win 'em all."

Other images I suggested were: her boss relaxing at home watering the lawn; cooking in the kitchen, with an apron on; answering his wife, "Yes, dear. Yes, dear."

D. Use GPE for Authority Figures

Because she still had some anxiety about authority figures, Lee then built a GPE hierarchy for authority figures:

SUD	SITUATION
30	Being told by a policeman to move her car
40	Asking a headwaiter in a fancy restaurant for a table
50	Going to see a big, busy medical specialist and explaining her problem to him
60	Talking to the chairman of the board at a cocktail party
70	Meeting the chairman in the dining room and sitting next to him
80	Going in and telling her boss about a new idea she has
90	Going into a meeting and answering questions from superiors about her new idea

Lee practiced relaxation exercises at home, and then exposed herself to the items in the hierarchy. It took her about ten sessions to finally feel comfortable with the most difficult scene. By the time she accepted the promotion most of her fears had been overcome. She worked well with her new boss in a positive atmosphere of mutual respect.

THE BOSS WHO HOLLERS: JULIE

During one of our group meetings for working women, Julie reported to the others that she was having a problem on her job. She had been going from company to company, and finally had found a good position as the assistant to the producer of a game show on a local TV station. He was a very exciting, high-powered person to work for, but whenever things didn't go exactly the way he wanted, he screamed at everyone, and Julie could feel her stomach get tied up in knots. Her whole body would stiffen up and she would feel like running away.

Her parents were very quiet, timid, fearful people of European extraction. Julie said she could remember her father being very apologetic and ingratiating to a policeman when he was ordered to pull over in the car, even when he hadn't done anything. His voice would quiver and he would visibly shrink. That image of her father stayed in her mind, and came back when she met loud authority figures. When she went to elementary and high school she was afraid of the teachers who were overbearing. So when her new boss yelled, even at other people, she was frightened. She felt she couldn't protect herself.

PROBLEM: Julie was easily upset whenever anyone yelled at her. She had a boss who kept his office staff off guard by yelling at them. She was suffering physically from the stress and feared she might have to quit a good job.

Solution

A. Evaluate Self-talk
Julie wrote down the messages she was giving herself when the boss yelled:

1. I'm always wrong.
2. He's going to fire me; he doesn't like my work.

She decided that these were irrational, and challenged them with rational statements:

IRRATIONAL	RATIONAL
1. I'm always wrong.	1. It's just his style, it's not me. He hollers at everybody. When he's not sure, he attacks.
2. He's going to fire me, he doesn't like my work.	2. He's given absolutely no indication that he's going to fire me.

B. Use GPE for Men Yelling or Talking Loudly
Because Julie had high anxiety about men raising their voices, I suggested she build a GPE hierarchy for men hollering, or talking loudly to her:

SUD	SITUATION
30	Parking her car, with the garage attendant yelling at her to move it
40	At an intersection, with a truckdriver yelling "Come on, lady, we don't have all day!"
50	The boss yelling at the whole office, including her, in a meeting
60	The boss yelling at her and one other employee for being late with an assignment

70 The boss hollering at her over the telephone for misplacing a memo he needs

90 The boss hollering at her, face to face, for giving him a report a half-hour late

C. Humanize the Boss

Julie imagined her boss sitting on the floor like a baby, having a tantrum. He was sitting there in a diaper, throwing things and hollering. She imagined herself looking at him with a little bit of contempt, calmly waiting for him to get over his tantrum.

If you have been getting anxious or have felt intimidated because you were giving a person more power in your mind than he should have, try humanizing the person using imagery, the way Julie did here. You might, for example, imagine your boss wheeling his children or grandchildren in a baby carriage, feeling very proud of them; see him stuck in an elevator, and nervous about it; see him being chewed out by *his* boss.

D. Learn Assertive Responses

I also had Julie practice some assertive responses so she wouldn't feel quite so helpless in the situation: "I know it's upsetting to you when things don't go right, but I can be much more helpful to you and function better when I don't feel you're yelling at me." Or, "I particularly appreciate it when things aren't going right and you speak to me calmly. It makes it easier for me to handle things effectively."

AWED BY AUTHORITY: BARBARA

Barbara was a sales rep for a small, prestigious textile firm. She enjoyed her job, but she always felt very uncomfortable talking to people in authority. She felt inferior and didn't think they would be interested in talking to her. She was comfortable with peers and customers, but if she had to give a report to anyone in a position superior to hers or chat with him she became very tense and anxious. She'd say what she had to say, become flustered, and then leave abruptly. Consequently, they thought of her as someone not to be taken seriously; they thought she was a lightweight. She thought: "They'll get tired of me quickly, or bored with me, so I'd better say what I have to say and leave."

PROBLEM: Barbara was so intimidated by authority figures that she couldn't talk comfortably with them. She acted like a frightened office girl instead of a woman with executive potential.

Solution

A. Evaluate Self-talk
Barbara first made a list of all the messages she was giving herself about the situation:

1. They're much smarter than I am.
2. They're much more important than I am.
3. They're much older and wouldn't be interested in what I have to say.
4. I never know what to say to them.

She decided these were all irrational statements and challenged them with rational ones:

IRRATIONAL	RATIONAL
1. They're much smarter than I am.	1. They're not much smarter than I am. They might have some specific knowledge I don't have but I can acquire that if I want. I

	may know more in other areas than they do.
2. They're much more important than I am.	2. Right at this moment they have a higher position but they didn't always. They had to work their way up, too. They didn't start up there.
3. They're much older and wouldn't be interested in what I have to day.	3. I may have some new ideas and new slants that they haven't thought about.
4. I never know what to say to them.	4. I can run over topics of conversation in my head before I speak to them. I can be myself; I can be natural without having people think I'm stepping out of line.

B. Learn New Skills

I suggested that Barbara read *How To Talk with Practically Anybody About Practically Anything*, an excellent book by Barbara Walters, with some wonderful pointers for people who feel they have trouble making conversation. I also discussed with her some of the power ploys that can be involved in conversation between men and women or between subordinate and boss. These you will find mentioned in Chapter Six.

C. Create a New Image

To have her perceive herself differently, and therefore act in a different way, I had Barbara create a positive image of herself. First she saw herself in the next job up, knowing the higher-ups, knowledgeable, and functioning on the same level as her boss. She saw herself dictating to her secretary, making direct eye contact, speaking in a calm voice, seated comfortably at her desk, calm, confident, and competent. In her imagination she filled in all the details—she knew how the office looked, exactly what she was working on. Then she imagined herself speaking on the telephone discussing a sales meeting with a vice-president, in a very professional tone.

D. Use a Model

I then asked Barbara to choose a woman she knew who was confident and successful and to pick up cues from her. She selected a woman high up in her company, a junior vice-president she respected and who came across with authority. Barbara then imagined herself acting in the same way and feeling the same self-assurance she imagined the woman felt. She copied the way she carried herself, the manner in which she spoke. The woman talked with a relaxed air of authority—as if she knew what she was talking about, because she'd researched her subject. Barbara imagined herself in this way until she was comfortable with the image.

E. Use Thought-stopping

As Barbara began to have longer conversations with her superiors at work, she sometimes still made negative comments to herself: "I really blew that"; "They'll think I'm stupid"; "I stood there like a dummy." So she used thought-stopping: Every time a negative thought occurred to her, she said to herself, "Stop!" and switched to a positive statement: "I understood what he was saying; next time if I want to respond I will." Then she reinforced the positive statement by thinking about a pleasant scene.

F. Praise Oneself

Every time Barbara had a conversation with a boss in real life, she reinforced herself: "I really handled that well. I came across as capable and intelligent."

Eventually Barbara was comfortable speaking to people in authority, and attracted a sponsor who helped her move ahead.

THE HARSH WOMAN BOSS: MARLENE

Marlene was promoted from executive secretary to lower management in a service company. As a supervisor, she didn't seem to know how to motivate people. She came to our women's group complaining she was disgusted with her job. She knew what she was doing and knew a lot about organizing people—more than the person before her—but her unit was just not doing their work. When people from other sections had dealings with her group, they said they'd prefer to deal with others besides her. She thought this was discrimination because she was a woman.

When I did role playing with Marlene, and acted as one of her subordinates, her whole personality changed. She assumed a dictatorial, imperious air. We taped the conversation, and I replayed it for her. Her mouth fell open: "Is that me?" she asked. "It sounds like Adolf Hitler." There was nothing courteous, humane, or pleasant about her. She was cold, dictatorial, uncompromising.

PROBLEM: Marlene was alienating people because of her dictatorial manner. As a result, morale was low in her department, and employee turnover was high.

Solution

A. Monitor Oneself

To help her get a clearer picture of what was happening at work, I suggested that Marlene tape-record herself for a day,

with her staff, secretary, associates, and people in other
departments. She soon saw that she was being too authoritarian.

B. Evaluate Self-Talk
Marlene then listed the statements she was making to herself:

1. If I'm nice, no one will listen to me.
2. This is the way you have to act when you're a boss.
3. I have to be on top of them or they'll walk all over me.
   They'll find out how weak I am if I give them a
   chance.
4. You've got to make people respect you.

She decided that the first three statements were irrational,
and challenged them with rational ones:

IRRATIONAL	RATIONAL
1. If I'm nice, no one will listen to me.	1. I can be firm and still be pleasant. Kindness is not weakness. Coldness is not strength.
2. This is the way you have to act when you're a boss.	2. There are many leadership styles. A secure boss isn't afraid to be nice.
3. I have to be on top of them or they'll walk all over me; they'll find out how weak I am.	3. This is not a power struggle. I'm in a position of authority that I earned and that speaks for itself.

The fourth statement was a rational one. Marlene took it a
step further and made it constructive:

4. You've got to make people   4. I want to be respected, not

respect you.

feared. When I give respect to others, I get respect from them.

C. Use a Model

I asked Marlene to pick another female manager in her company who got things done, and had authority, and a style different from hers. She chose the manager in the next department who was quiet and firm and very popular. She had a lot of authority and got respect because she showed others respect, and conveyed a clear idea of what she expected of them. She had created a productive ambience in her office, where people helped one another.

D. Create a New Image

Marlene needed to develop real leadership quality, to see herself as a leader, as the head of a unit, and to take it for granted that what she requested was what people were going to do. In imagery she saw herself as the leader, calmly stating her ideas and how she would like them worked out. She saw herself explaining to a subordinate that he would have to finish a small clerical task in a way she preferred. She explained it calmly, but firmly, fully expecting to be obeyed.

She saw herself answering a subordinate who had asked for vacation time when it wasn't convenient: "I understand it's a better time for you, and I wish I could arrange for it, but I really need you here to handle the unfinished accounts. I'd like you take it in July instead of August."

E. Learn Assertive Skills

Marlene learned appropriate assertive techniques to take the place of aggressive responses. She first saw herself practicing various assertive responses in imagery. She imagined herself telling a subordinate to finish a report on time when he said he couldn't get it in. She saw herself responding with empathy: "I understand, but I'd like you to finish this report by Monday. I know it will be inconvenient for you, and I do understand the situation, but I do need this done by tomorrow." Eventually she practiced assertive responses by role playing with a friend.

Gradually the morale in Marlene's department improved, because she was able to develop a more acceptable leadership style. By learning to be appropriately assertive and to eliminate her aggressive, dictatorial style, she got the cooperation she needed, and developed good rapport with her co-workers.

12 ── NURTURING

Nurturing is a common trait in women because women are reinforced for taking care of people. It's a complex situation because the nurturer encourages people to be dependent on her, and then becomes dependent on them because it makes her feel needed, useful, and valuable. In this way she doesn't develop any sense of her own independence or respect for herself in any capacity other than caretaker, one who helps and serves others. Therefore, she's vulnerable to rejection as a nurturer because all her security lies in the fact that others need her.

In some occupations—nurse, social worker, or mother—nurturing can be an asset, but in the business world it's inappropriate, and often harmful to a woman's career. You can learn how to curb your nurturing instincts without feeling you are being cruel. You can also change your self-image from protective big sister or mother to understanding executive woman.

THE OFFICE MOTHER: ANNE

Anne, thirty-five, was an only child born to a couple in their middle years. As a youngster she frequently played the parental role to her mother and father. They gradually leaned on her more and more. After they died, she decided to go into the business world, and got a good job as assistant to the employee relations coordinator for the transportation division of a large oil company. By the time she came to see me, she had been working seven years, and during the first three had had two promotions. In the office she had several people working under her in a clerical capacity, who kept coming to her unable to do their jobs. Feeling protective of them, she did part of their work for them. She was known as the office mother, and everyone came to her with their problems. Despite the fact that she was well liked at the office and was efficient at her job, four years went by and she received no promotion. This greatly disturbed her. She saw people who were once her subordinates rising above her on the corporate ladder. When she mentioned this to her boss, he said she was very nice but did not quite fit his idea of the executive image.

Anne had to realize that it was very important for her to be valued and that people appealing to her for help fed her sense of worth. Nurturing people made them depend on her; it made her feel needed. She believed she was being cold when she turned people down.

PROBLEM: By continually attending to the personal needs of her co-workers, Anne was projecting an unprofessional image of herself and failing to develop her executive potential.

Solution

A. Evaluate Self-talk

Anne first made a list of the statements she was making to herself about helping people:

1. My co-worker will fall on his face if I don't help him.
2. If I don't help him he'll fail.
3. He won't like me if I don't help him. It will be unbearable!

Then she challenged these irrational statements with rational ones:

IRRATIONAL	RATIONAL
1. My co-worker will fall on his face if I don't help him.	1. By allowing him to do it himself, I am allowing him to learn and build his self-confidence.
2. If I don't help him he'll fail.	2. He will be stronger if he does it himself. By taking his responsibility I'm not letting him develop his own ability and self-esteem.
3. He won't like me if I don't help him. It will be unbearable!	3. He may be angry at me for a while. He'll get over it. I'm not here to win a popularity contest. I'm here to get the job done in the best, reasonable manner. If I continue doing his work, he'll end up not liking me anyway, because I'm taking away his self-respect.

B. Learn Assertive Responses

I suggested that Anne learn some of the assertive techniques discussed in Chapter Five. I asked her to read the books recommended on assertion. With a friend, Anne practiced saying no to requests that were inappropriate or excessive.

C. Build New Skills

Anne took a workshop on management organization. Then she began to teach her subordinates how to approach and organize a job:

- To see the job as a whole
- To organize it into workable components, break it down into steps, on paper if necessary
- To work on one aspect at a time

She made it clear that the end result was their responsibility.

D. Use a Model

Next, Anne used a role model, someone who was moving up the corporate ladder. She picked an executive in the company whom she respected and watched how he operated. She saw he didn't get to the top by worrying about whether or not people loved him. He was considerate of other people's needs, but his primary concern was doing what was right for the business. She said to herself: "Mr. So-and-so didn't get where he is by trying to please everybody."

E. Create a New Image

In imagery Anne created a picture of herself as a person comfortable being in a position of authority. She was handling people, being efficient, encouraging of others in their work, engendering confidence in people and motivating them.

THE DEN MOTHER: CAROLINE

Caroline was an attractive woman in her late forties who went back to work after she'd raised a family. She was administrative assistant to a vice-president of a retail firm. He was young enough to be her son, and most members of the department were the age of her children—and that's how Caroline saw them. She kept a box of cookies on her desk, and was always ready for a sympathetic chat. Most of the younger people soon developed the habit of dropping into her office to talk. She didn't have time to keep up with her work because she was so busy solving their problems. She loved her job and enjoyed the feeling of being accepted and needed by the whole office. But a difficulty arose when she got a notice that her work was falling below standard, and she was missing deadlines. Letters were piling up on her desk. She knew she was behind in her work, but was shocked when she was given a warning that if her work didn't improve she was going to be dismissed.

PROBLEM: Caroline's behavior in the office was not businesslike. She was inappropriately mothering. The job was filling an emotional gap in Caroline's life; it was a replacement for her family. She had to separate work in the office from her emotional needs.

Solution

A. Assess the Situation

Caroline ranked high in nurturing on her behavior questionnaire. I had her keep a diary of what she did during the day and of her interactions in the office. She recorded how much time was allotted for each task. She soon noticed that a lot of time was being spent talking to people about personal things; her work was constantly being interrupted. Then she saw the need for more consistent stretches of time devoted to work, and planned to do her socializing during her lunch hour and after work.

B. Evaluate Self-talk

Caroline then made a list of statements she was making to herself:

1. As long as I'm taking care of them they'll like me.
2. I'm not enough by myself.
3. If I do favors for them, they'll accept me.
4. I'll attract people if I help them.

For the irrational statements she substituted rational ones:

IRRATIONAL	RATIONAL
1. As long as I'm taking care of them they'll like me.	1. People will like me for what I am. I don't have to take care of them for them to like me.
2. I'm not enough by myself.	2. There are many things about me people can like.
3. If I do favors for them, they'll accept me. Al-though there was some truth to her fourth statement, it would not lead to appropriate behavior. She countered it with a more productive statement:	3. If I do favors for them, they'll exploit me.
4. I'll attract people if I help them.	4. Yes, but I'll attract them for the wrong reason.

C. Learn Assertive Skills

Like Anne, Caroline learned the assertiveness techniques discussed in Chapter Five. She practiced making assertive statements in imagery. Soon, when someone came into her office to start a personal conversation, she was able to give friendly but short answers and tell them in a firm but pleasant way she had a deadline to meet or other work to do: "Look, why don't we meet after work and talk about it?" Or, "I really want to discuss this with you, but this is not a good time. How about going over it at lunch?" Or, "That's a problem that deserves a lot of thought. But this isn't a good time. How about meeting after work so we can really get into it."

D. Create a New Self-image

Caroline realized that her mothering role, rewarding as it may have been, was not going to help her get ahead in the business world. She needed to develop a new identity. I suggested that she see herself in imagery, functioning efficiently, in charge, and being respected for doing a competent job. She saw herself in her office, well groomed, sitting behind her desk discussing a work assignment with a colleague. She imagined herself being businesslike, getting respect from the boss, and being accepted by others as a peer. She imagined Alice, a colleague, coming into her office, and starting to talk about her ex-husband. Caroline very nicely says, "I can see why you're very upset about this. Why don't we have lunch and talk about it?"

In the image she created, her office was neat and uncluttered. On her desk there was a telephone, a desktop calendar, a small, framed family picture, an outgoing-incoming file box, and several neatly piled folders she was working on. The atmosphere in her office was informal but orderly. She saw herself planning projects and organizing her schedules. If someone interrupted, she said, "I have this to finish, can I get back to you?" People were relating to her in a still friendly, but more respectful manner.

E. Make a List of Assets

To broaden her image of herself, I asked her to make a list of her competencies. She wrote down: Bright, attractive, enthusiastic, warm, efficient, good at math, organized, speak fluent Spanish.

F. Learn New Skills

Caroline had to become more independent and get involved in the outside world. She joined a health club and played racquet ball. She became involved in activities that didn't require nurturing, so she could begin to see herself in another light. Then she joined a women's group, which reinforced her identity as a working woman. She worked on increasing her social activities, so that work didn't take the place of a social life, and developed social skills that led to a more interesting social life that included her husband and some new friends who were professional people.

Eventually Caroline was able to set limits for herself and others on the socializing that went on in her office. Her office behavior became more businesslike, still, her friends at work valued her advice and, because she wasn't as available as before, respected her even more.

THE RESCUER: SARAH

Sarah is the oldest of six children. While she was growing up her parents worked, so when any of the children—especially her ailing younger brother—had trouble, they came to her. Because her parents were busy, she had to be a surrogate parent. Her younger brother was constantly needing her care. When she finished high school she went to work for an insurance company in a low-skill clerical job. She was always very helpful to everyone around her. At the age of thirty she got married. After five years the marriage hadn't worked out, and she went back to school to learn more skills in order to get a better job than her last one.

Ultimately she got a position in the personnel department of a small competitive service company. Her co-worker, Mark, was a charming young man, but he had a drinking problem. He was neglecting his assignments and sometimes didn't even show up for work. She began covering for him. At first he showed a great deal of appreciation, and said she was changing his life. He'd promise each time it would be the last time, and that he'd shape up. She ended up doing two jobs: all of hers and half of his. Finally, when she told him she couldn't do it anymore, he became verbally abusive. Still, she was afraid not to help him because she knew he'd lose his job and she'd feel guilty. Eventually they stopped being friends. His drinking become common knowledge, and he was fired.

At the end of the year, Sarah was promoted to assistant personnel manager. Her tendency to be a rescuer began to get her into trouble. When it came to hiring, she put résumés aside and let her intuition rule. Hardship took precedence over merit. She began to hire applicants more because they needed their jobs and because their sad stories moved her, than because they were qualified. It was just as hard for her to fire incompetent employees after they told her about their personal problems. As a result, the quality of work for the whole company began to slip, customers started to complain, and the president called for a review of employees in all departments. He also called for an investigation of the hiring and firing policies of the personnel department. Sarah was shocked when she was given notice that she was being transferred to another department—a much less prestigious position.

PROBLEM: Sarah was a rescuer. When she didn't rush in to help people she felt upset and anxious. Emotional needs were interfering with company needs.

Solution

A. Evaluate Self-talk

Sarah had to redefine "helping." She had to see that *doing* things for a person robs them of the chance to learn. *Helping* means teaching or guiding them in such a way that they learn and grow. It is respecting their potential for growth.

Sarah made a list of the messages she was giving herself about situations in which she was nurturing:

1. This person needs help.
2. If I don't help him, no one else will.
3. I'll make an exception just this time. He'll shape up later. He won't let me down. If I give him a chance, he'll pull through.

She decided that two of these statements were rational and one was irrational. She challenged the irrational one with a rational statement:

IRRATIONAL

3. I'll make an exception just this time. He'll shape up later. He won't let me down. If I give him a chance, he'll pull through.

RATIONAL

3. I'm not being realistic. A good yardstick of a person's future behavior is his past behavior.

For the rational statements, she came up with alternative ones that would lead her to more productive behavior:

RATIONAL

1. This person needs help.

PRODUCTIVE

1. True, he needs help. And the best way I can help him is to let him face reality, find out that he needs skills, and do something about getting them.

2. If I don't help him, no one else will.

2. That may be so, and it would be for the best. I can tell him where to get the information and then he'll learn. He'll help him-

self. He'll gradually learn to handle situations on his own. In that way his confidence and self-respect will grow.

B. Practice Not Nurturing in Imagery

More than anything else, Sarah needed practice responding differently to situations in which she used to feel that she had to offer help. She needed to curb her impulse to rush in and offer assistance. She simply wasn't used to saying no, even when saying no was appropriate. I had her imagine herself in the following situations:

- A panhandler approaches her on the street, and she shakes her head and keeps on walking.
- At a meeting her boss asks if someone will work on the weekend to finish a report. Sarah sits quietly and waits for someone else to volunteer.
- She sees a hungry stray dog or cat on the street and passes them by.
- She gives a memo to a secretary to type, and the secretary says with a pained look, "I hope you don't want this right now." Sarah replies, "Unfortunately, I do need it right away."
- At lunch one of her colleagues remarks to the group: "I really could use some help on my tax return," and glances at Sarah. She lets it go by without answering.
- A job interviewee says he needs the job to pay off his debts and pay for his children's school, and she doesn't hire him because his skills are inadequate.

C. Learn Assertive Skills

Because Sarah needed to learn assertive responses, we practiced some of the techniques described in Chapter Five. We role played situations that gave her a chance to practice saying no.

D. Practice Not Nurturing in Real Life
When Sarah had mastered the assertive techniques and felt comfortable with the scenes in imagery, we role played them in the office.

E. Praise Oneself
Every time Sarah handled a situation well in real life, she remembered to praise herself with statements like: "I helped him to learn that." "I did well allowing him to take care of himself." She even rewarded herself with small treats for handling certain situations in an appropriate way.

13

BEING A PERFECTIONIST

Many women in business believe that if they do a perfect job their boss will think more of them and promote them. That isn't always the case. Trying to do a *perfect* job creates problems. When you become a perfectionist you limit yourself by doing a few jobs perfectly instead of many jobs well. You become overspecialized; you lose your flexibility. You invest too much time in doing one job well, and lose your perspective in reaching out and preparing yourself for the next job that's to come.

You may get away with being a perfectionist if you are training to become a diamond cutter or master silversmith, but not if you want to move up the corporate management ladder. If you are a manager you need to be flexible. You have to know where to invest your time. You have to know how to rank the importance for various tasks. Perfectionism frequently shows itself as a problem in time management. It's important that you set priorities and structure time to increase productivity.

As girls, women have been taught to do every little thing perfectly. Many of us, without being aware of it, tend to be myopic. We focus on the task at hand, without looking at the long-range goal. This doesn't work in business, where growth and success call for a broader vision.

NOT ABLE TO DELEGATE WORK: DANIELLE

Danielle is the only child of a very demanding mother who was widowed when Danielle was twenty-two. She attended a community college but continued to live at home with her parents. Afterward, she took a graduate degree in accounting, but didn't finish because her father died and she had to work to help support her mother. Her mother was a perfectionist. Danielle was very orderly and had an excellent record in school. Still, no matter how she tried she felt she never could live up to her mother's standards. She could never please her.

Eventually Danielle became a supervisor in the accounting department of a prestigious but conservative retailing firm. She ran into trouble because she felt that everything leaving her department had to be perfect. She thought she had to be on top of every job because somebody else would mess it up. If anything came out of her unit that wasn't perfect she felt very anxious. As a result she wouldn't delegate authority, and she ended up doing most of the work herself. She had to personally check every balance sheet and cost analysis. She managed to do this most of the year, but when there was a lot of work to be done, she found she couldn't possibly do all the tasks herself. Yet she was unwilling to entrust them to someone else. The stress was becoming more than she could handle.

When I met Danielle, she was dressed in a very controlled

way, trim and tailored, with not a hair out of place. She said she had always secretly envied the women in her office who were more flamboyant. She simply couldn't bring herself to emulate them. Danielle was brought up so rigidly she was afraid to take chances. She had to be perfect in every way.

PROBLEM: Danielle had difficulty delegating work because she felt no one else would do it according to her high standards. She was overburdening herself with unnecessary details and creating a situation she could no longer cope with.

Solution

A. Evaluate Self-talk

Danielle first made a list of all the messages she was giving herself about the situation:

1. You can't trust anybody to do anything.
2. I feel best when I know I've done a perfect job. I should do every job perfectly, or not at all.
3. I can do it better than they can do it.
4. I have more control over it if I do it myself.

She recognized the irrationality of the first two statements and disputed them with rational ones:

IRRATIONAL	RATIONAL
1. You can't trust anybody to do anything.	1. There are competent people, and I got competent by doing things, so will they. I'm certainly not the only competent person around.
2. I feel best when I know I've done a perfect job. I	2. There's no such thing as perfection. I would like to

should do every job per- do a good job.
fectly, or not at all.

Although her last two statements were not irrational, they
would in time, lead to unproductive behavior. She found productive responses to them.

RATIONAL	PRODUCTIVE
3. I can do it better than they can do it.	3. That may be so. But if I do everything then I'm limited in the amount of things I can get out of this department.
4. I have more control over it if I do it myself.	4. Fine, but I'm limited. I can get good work by doing good supervision. If I'm able to supervise and use my time correctly I can get more work done and still end up with a good result.

B. Use GPE for Delegating Work

Because she had some anxiety about delegating tasks to
others, Danielle built a GPE hierarchy for delegating work.

SUD	SITUATION
25	Having someone make a phone call for her
30	Having her secretary schedule all her appointments for a week while she's away on vacation
45	Having someone write a letter for her, and she signs it
50	Having someone finish a cost-estimate report for her
65	Letting a letter be mailed that a subordinate says is okay

80   Having a subordinate do important calculations and show her only the totals

100   Having someone else deal with a new account

C. Use GPE for Not Being Perfect

After she felt more comfortable delegating authority, we used a GPE hierarchy for not being perfect.

SUD	SITUATION
10	Leaving the bed unmade and the dishes un-washed
20	Going out with a spot on her dress
30	Being ten minutes late for an appointment
40	Forgetting to call someone back
50	Forgetting an appointment
75	Giving someone wrong instructions
80	With a 10:00 A.M. deadline for a memo, letting the memo go out with a misspelling because it's two minutes to ten.
100	Not finishing a report by a deadline

Then she followed the GPE hierarchy for delegating work in real life, and reinforced herself for it by praising herself each time she completed one of the steps on the hierarchy. She used phrases like: "Very good. This is a good way to make the department more productive." Soon Danielle was at ease letting her subordinates do their own work, and had more time to devote to management.

DOING EVERYTHING PERFECTLY: ARLENE

Arlene was the eldest child of three. Her mother died when she was seven, and so she learned at an early age to take over many of the household duties. As she grew older she took pride in running a meticulous home for a demanding father. She managed to put herself through a local business school and got a job in the consumer relations department of a large manufacturing firm. She was competent and took pride in her work. She prepared reports, in-house material, and advertising copy with a great deal of care. Before long, however, she became obsessed with doing a perfect job. She began taking paperwork home at night. She was spending more time than necessary on the work trying to make it "perfect." Eventually her work dominated her every waking hour; she had no time to do anything else. It was her world, she had almost no other interests. By the time she came to see me she was so overworked that her health had begun to deteriorate. She was in a state of exhaustion and confusion.

PROBLEM: Arlene needed to examine her priorities. She asked herself: What do I want? What are my goals? What is more important, doing a perfect job, or advancing my career? What will do me good? What will give me visibility? She had to decide what she wanted.

Solution

A. Evaluate Self-talk

Arlene got in touch with some of the thoughts that went with her drive for perfection. She recognized their irrational and limiting qualities, and challenged them with rational statements:

IRRATIONAL	RATIONAL
1. I'm the kind of person who does everything perfectly. I can't help it. That's the way I do things; that's the way I am.	1. That's not the way I "am." That's how I have gotten into the habit of doing things. I can change the way I do things. I can develop new, more productive habits.

2. The way to get ahead is to do your job better than anyone else.

2. The way to get ahead is to do a good job *and* prepare myself for the next step up. It's important to keep my flexibile perspective. A person who gets ahead is confident, competent, and flexible. She sees her job as one of a series of steps upward.

B. Use GPE for Doing Everything Perfectly

I also gave Arlene a GPE hierarchy for doing everything perfectly, so she wouldn't put as much energy into tasks at work. Her hierarchy was very much like the one Danielle used.

If, like Arlene, you have a problem with needing to do everything perfectly, you might ask yourself some of the same questions. What's more important, doing a particular chore perfectly or the overall picture of doing your job adequately and moving toward a goal? Like Arlene, you may need to practice some time planning. Look at time spent as an investment. Think, "I'll invest myself in this and it will pay off."

EXPECTING EVERYONE ELSE TO BE PERFECT: ELIZABETH

Elizabeth and her two younger sisters were raised by unhappily married parents in a cluttered, disorderly home. Her mother was impulsive; her father was undependable. In her house things never were planned, they just seemed to happen. Whenever she wanted something for school she could never depend on her parents to give it to her. She began at a very early age to keep her own world very orderly, as a means of survival. She developed precise personal habits, which gave her life structure. The more disorganized life around her became the more she focused on her own meticulous world to escape the chaos she was living in.

At school, the clean logic of math appealed to her. She went on to business school and studied accounting. She was married for four years, but the marriage didn't work out and she was amicably divorced. Then she got a job in the accounting department of a national discount carpet chain, as a bookkeeper. She did brilliantly, and her boss often complimented her. She enjoyed working on figures; when her balance sheets came out perfectly, it gave her an enjoyable feeling of completeness. Her books always balanced. Elizabeth's boss was impressed by her competence and intelligence, and decided to promote her to a supervisory position. He said she inspired his confidence with the high quality of her work, and with her orderliness and accuracy. But after six months it was clear that as a supervisor Elizabeth was not very successful. In her new position she was as demanding of her subordinates as she was of herself. Everything they did had to be perfect. When they couldn't meet her standards, she became critical. She believed her way was the right way—the only way.

It wasn't long before her department suffered from low morale and high turnover. Her department was jokingly known as Siberia. The job was very important to her, but it seemed that the harder she tried, the more things went wrong. She could accept her subordinates' work only if it was perfect, but few employees were able to tolerate her detailed criticism. They became resistant and uncooperative, and the department ran inefficiently. She became frustrated and irritable. By the time she came to see me, she was almost in danger of losing her job. When I met her she seemed to be a very controlled and together woman, tailored and precise, an intelligent brunette with an alert look about her.

PROBLEM: When she was a bookkeeper Elizabeth's perfectionism was an asset. As a manager, she had unrealistic expectations that the people who worked for her would be perfect. She was too demanding of her subordinates.

Solution

A. Evaluate Self-talk
I asked Elizabeth to make note of the statements she was making to herself about the situation. They were:

1. All the incompetents are working for me.
2. Everyone in my department is a poor worker, or else I'm a bad manager.

These were judgements and observations that later would have to be checked out in reality.

B. Monitor Oneself
To get a clearer picture of what was happening at work, I had Elizabeth record in a diary and on tape her activities and personal interactions at work. The written diary kept track of the conversations she had with others: the subjects of the conversations as well as what her feelings were during them. For example:

10:00 A.M.   Meeting with Maryanne and Doreen about lateness of the staff. Also discussed staff meeting. Felt frustrated because they didn't seem as disturbed about a new employee's lateness as I was.

2:00 P.M.   Discussed quarterly increase with a subordinate and reminded her it wasn't automatic. She seemed hostile. Told her her work could be neater. Felt frustrated because she didn't seem to care if she had typed all the orders or handwritten them quickly.

After a week, Elizabeth and I went over the diary together and listened to the tape. She was then easily able to evaluate her own behavior. It was clear to her that most of her remarks to subordinates were critical ones. She also saw that the most common feelings she had during a workday were frustration and dissatisfaction about the level of work in her department.

She wondered whether all the company's incompetents had been put in her department or if her expectations were unrealistic. To find this out, I suggested she try some reality testing.

C. Assess Situation

Elizabeth spent some time observing the employees in other departments, particularly in production, which had recently won an award for high output. She saw three things that became the focus of our therapy. She noticed that the employees in production were just as competent as the ones in her department, neither more nor less. She saw just as much "inefficiency" there as in her own department. And she noticed that the interactions between the boss and the employees in the production department were almost always positive, comfortable ones. This made her realize that her expectations were too high.

D. Make Positive Statements

Elizabeth started using positive statements to herself. When she found herself in a situation where she was being perfectionistic:

1. This work is good, it's better than most. I'm satisfied. What's next?
2. If I hold everything up until it's perfect, I'll never get anything done.

3. I'm doing my best, they're doing their best. I'm satisfied. I know I'm efficient and competent.
4. High morale makes for good performance. If I praise good work they'll do more of it for me.

Soon she was comfortable accepting work with minor, unimportant flaws.

E. Use a Model

I asked Elizabeth to pick someone in the company she admired, who seemed to have a good relationship with her subordinates, to use as a model. She chose the division manager in production, because she saw her department had high output and her staff liked and respected her. She soon observed that she was quick to compliment her subordinates when they did good work. She pointed out errors when she noticed them, but didn't dwell on them. She seemed to expect high performance of her staff, yet she did not criticize or punish. Elizabeth tried, like her, to take a positive approach: to reward the positive and ignore the negative. It got good results, and within two months her department's morale had improved a great deal.

EXPECTING SELF-PERFECTION: LONNIE

Lonnie grew up in an affluent suburb. At school she was always at the top of her class. Her compositions and papers were frequently mounted on the school bulletin board as examples of excellent work. Her parents bragged about her, and Lonnie loved the attention. She felt very special. Her father always said, "Lonnie will never let us down."

All went well until she reached college. There the work was more difficult and the professors more demanding. Even when she did an excellent job she didn't stand out because there were other people just as good as she was. She started spending more and more time on each paper, hoping to win recognition. As a result, she couldn't keep up with other assignments and began handing in papers late, and in some cases even failed to complete them at all. By her senior year she had accumulated so many incompletes that she was unable to graduate with her class. Naturally, this was a great disappointment to her parents and she began to doubt her ability and felt guilty about letting her family down. She spent another year making up her incompletes and finally graduated.

Lonnie was attractive, articulate, and sophisticated. After college she began as a management trainee with a large corporation, but quit before the program was finished. She then went from one job to another, always starting with a lot of enthusiasm and staying just long enough to get to the point where promotion could be expected, and then quit. She went from automotive import to clothing import to car rentals, always showing great promise in the beginning, but never following through. When she'd been there long enough and it was time for promotions to be given out, she'd get very anxious and think, "This job isn't for me," and she'd find some minor excuse to quit. But she wanted to work. She came to me very confused.

PROBLEM: Lonnie had been unable to stay with one job and develop a career. She delayed things, trying to make them perfect, and she was a quitter. She was afraid she would fail by being proven imperfect. If she couldn't be perfect, she wouldn't play.

Each time Lonnie quit a job, she saved herself from being put in the position of either not getting the promotion or getting it and possibly failing at it. In this way she avoided damaging her perfectionistic self-image. Rather than face the fact that she was not perfect, she stopped before proving herself imperfect. She thought: "Doing things perfectly makes me feel secure." The flawless image of herself that she tried to fulfill was unrealistic.

Solution

A. Explore Belief System

Lonnie believed she had to be perfect in any job from the very beginning. She didn't take learning into account. The learning process consists of practice and trial and error. She didn't realize that learning means gradually getting better. To get somewhere you have to make mistakes and then learn, and that's the way you develop. No one does anything new perfectly.

She also believed that successful people never made mistakes. I asked her to observe the people around her and be aware of the mistakes they made. She thought of her boss, and could remember several rather large errors he had made. When I pointed this out to her, she was able to see that some of her beliefs were irrational. She had thought:

1. Successful people never make mistakes, because they're perfect.
2. If I'm perfect, I'll be an immediate success.

Because Lonnie thought if she did a perfect job she'd be successful immediately, she grew anxious when she wasn't quickly rewarded or praised.

B. Evaluate Self-talk

Lonnie made a list of the statements she was making to herself:

1. If I don't do it correctly right away, I don't belong in the business.
2. I can't make a mistake, it's not allowed. I should be perfect.
3. I get upset when I make mistakes.

She then decided that two of these messages were unrealistic and challenged them with positive realistic ones.

UNREALISTIC	REALISTIC
1. If I don't do it correctly right away, I don't belong in the business.	1. When they're learning no one does it perfectly.
2. I can't make a mistake, it's not allowed. I should be perfect.	2. I learn by doing and by making mistakes. We learn more from our mistakes than our successes. The goal is to learn and grow. The doing and becoming are more important than the product.

She decided the third statement was realistic, and made it more productive:

3. I get upset when I make mistakes.	3. Yes, it's upsetting when I make mistakes, but I can give myself permission to make mistakes in order to learn.

C. Use GPE for Not Being Perfect

Lonnie found it hard to accept the fact that she could make mistakes in order to learn. So I asked her to build a GPE hierarchy for being imperfect, and to experience it in imagery.

I also asked her to make realistic, positive coping statements to herself about not being perfect in these situations.

SUD	SITUATION
30	Taking on a small task she doesn't know if she can handle and not being able to do it. *Coping statement:* Alex did the same thing, and he's pretty good.
40	Making a phone call, and calling a man by the wrong name—calling Mr. Braun Mr. Brown. *Coping statement:* I deal with a lot of people every day, and I'm bound to get some of their names wrong.
50	Making a wrong decision: She lets her secretary have Tuesday off and Tuesday's a very busy day. *Coping statement:* A decision had to be made quickly and I made it.
60	Giving an estimate of car sizes for branches, and making a small error in calculation so she ends up with too many big cars, and needing more economy cars. *Coping Statement:* I'm learning. Good try. I learned from that. If I did it all right I wouldn't have to be here learning. I'd be in charge of the whole department if I knew it all.

D. Create a New Image

Because Lonnie thought she could only be effective if she could be perfect, she had a distorted view of herself. She had a lot of skills and accomplishments, but she was overlooking them in striving for perfection. She had been reinforced only for being perfect. So she began to give herself praise for trying rather than succeeding. "Good try" and "I learned a lot from that."

Lonnie had never been criticized, so even a breath of criticism would floor her. She began to see criticism as part of the learning process, and to experience it as constructive. She had to seek it out at first in small matters. "Is there any way I could have done this better?" "Do you see how I could have improved this?" Since the idea of doing this made her anxious, she did it first in imagery, then eventually in real life.

Before too long Lonnie was much more tolerant of her own imperfections and mistakes. She started another management program, and when I last saw her, she was doing very well.

COMPETITION AND TEAMWORK

14

In unity there's strength. Teamwork means working with others for the good of all. Working in a corporate structure requires an ability to cooperate and be part of a whole. Women, because they have had one-to-one friendships as girls and little experience being on teams, haven't developed the skills that come from being on a team and which are essential in business; therefore they tend to operate as loners.

But, as we discussed earlier, men know what's appropriate in business: working together, getting along with people, getting respect, being effective. Men can work with people they don't like or wouldn't associate with socially, but they aren't threatened by it. They know they have to respect and follow the coaches—their superiors. They plan ahead and know the rules, which you can bend by being clever. They know if you get knocked down you get up and try again.

Women tend to be idealistic. They're taught that being right and being fair and honest will help them succeed. Women often see competition not as a chance to prove themselves but as a threatening rivalry, a contest against other women. But men see competition as a game with the possibility of gaining something. The main goal of competition is enjoying the stimulation of it, with the attitude that no one wins them all, but that it's exciting to try.

NEEDING TO BE RIGHT: BETTY

Betty was in a sales meeting with her boss and a customer when a disagreement developed over the cut of a certain footwear model that had been shipped. The customer complained to Betty, "This vamp is cut much too low. It is definitely *not* what I had specified." He was right. He had approved the original model Betty had presented, but subsequently her boss had suggested she modify the cut. Trying to absolve herself, she turned to her boss and said, "Don't you remember, you suggested it?" There was an embarrassed silence, then the boss sided with the customer. "He's right, Betty, it *is* cut too low. You shouldn't have let the order go through that way." The subject was changed. Later when she walked out of the meeting her boss avoided her glance and started talking to someone else. After a few weeks she noticed his attitude toward her had changed: He was cool.

Betty's need to be right also antagonized many of her coworkers. She often argued about unimportant matters in an effort to prove her point, to prove that she alone was right.

PROBLEM: Betty needed to be right. That was more important to her than being part of, and giving support to, the team. Betty had to learn that when you're working your way up in a corporation, harmonious relations are more important than being right. The unwritten law is: Don't question the coach or make the team look bad in front of others. Betty was losing more than she was gaining, winning the battles but losing the war. Eventually people didn't want to cooperate with her. She was alienating herself from her team.

Solution

A. Explore Belief System

I suggested Betty examine her belief system. Her underlying belief was: "To get ahead, I've got to be right." She had to learn discretion. There are situations in business that require diplomacy. I asked her, "Were you helping yourself or hindering yourself? How did the boss feel? Do you think he liked you more for it?" Her goal is not to show everyone how smart she is, but rather to show how much she contributes toward the success of the team or organization.

B. Practice Curbing Impetuosity in Imagery

Betty had to learn to weigh the situation before she spoke by asking herself, "If I say this, will the consequences be good or bad?" She practiced this in imagery. She saw herself about to correct a sales rep who had misquoted a projected sales figure. She stopped herself, and immediately rewarded herself by saying, "That's a smart thing to do—keep your cool. The overall job is more important than being right. It's not important for me to be right. It's more important to get along with the organization. I'll gain more in the long run than by being right." Gradually she came to understand the need for diplomatic behavior. When she found herself in a situation where she impulsively wanted to show she was right, she said to herself, "Stop! What will the effect of my words be?" and she rewarded herself with a positive statement, such as "That was a better thing to do. I left everybody feeling good about themselves."

C. Practice Being on a Team in Imagery

Betty needed to see herself as part of a team. I had her tune in to any team or club member experiences she may have had in her childhood, to get in touch with the feeling of unity she had when she was part of a team—part of something bigger than herself.

Betty made positive statements to herself about being part of a team: "It's a wonderful feeling to belong to a team. The whole is greater than the sum of its parts. I have much more strength as a member of a team than if I'm alone." In the image she developed the feeling of having other people for her, and being for them; not having to fight the battles all by herself. "Somebody will pick up the ball if I drop it."

D. Learn a New Skill

I also suggested she learn a team sport and join a club or softball team, where she could experience the good feeling of working with others and the sense of belonging. She did this in imagery: She saw herself enjoying the camaraderie, sharing the pride of winning, and finding the team enthusiasm contagious. She made positive statements to herself: "It's really fun to be part of a team. Win or lose, you always have support in your team members." Soon after, she joined a women's softball team made up of upwardly mobile women in management like herself.

If you haven't had much team experience as a girl it might be beneficial for you to join a team, such as your company's softball team, or become active in a political campaign or community project that interests you. Through these types of organized and collaborative efforts, you get a feeling of belonging.

WORKING WITH EVERYONE:
JESSICA

Women are frequently choosy about their associates and feel they can't work with people they don't like or respect. Men can relate to others in business even if they don't like them. They seem able to put personal feelings aside and collaborate with others, if only to achieve their goals.

Jessica was on the research staff of a news show for a TV network. She didn't like one of the older researchers. She found him abrasive. As one of the senior researchers in charge of foreign news, he was in a powerful position. She was a beginner, an assistant. Because she didn't like him or feel comfortable with him she avoided working with him whenever possible. Consequently she found herself being relegated more and more to the routine stories, while the more interesting ones were assigned to her fellow researchers.

PROBLEM: Jessica didn't want to work with someone she didn't like. She avoided a boss she disliked and disapproved of, and, as a result, alienated him. She was confusing a business relationship with a social one.

Solution

A. Evaluate Self-talk

I asked Jessica to make a list of the messages she was giving herself about the situation:

1. I can only work with people I like.
2. I can't work with that man: I can't tolerate his personality.
3. He acts crude and conceited.

Jessica operated on the faulty assumption that nothing productive could possibly come from working with a person you didn't like. At my suggestion she sorted out which of the statements she was making to herself were unrealistic and challenged them with realistic, positive ones:

UNREALISTIC	REALISTIC
1. I can only work with people I like.	1. It's more pleasant to work with people I like. It's what I prefer. But if I have

to I can work with others. Even though it may not be as pleasant, I can function just as well.

2. I can't work with that man; I can't tolerate his personality.

2. He's a business associate and he's a step to getting what I want. I don't have to approve of him to work with him. This is just part of the job.

She decided the third statement was realistic and turned it into a productive one:

REALISTIC	PRODUCTIVE
3. He acts crude and conceited.	3. That's how I perceive him. What's important is that I can learn a lot from him.

I asked her to think of him as a means to an end, a step in reaching the goal she had set for herself. Using positive self-statements like "I don't have to approve of him to work with him," helped her to distance herself, to see him as an associate, not someone who had to appeal to her as a friend.

B. Humanize the Person

I suggested that she humanize her senior colleague, see his other sides, view him in a more humane light. She told herself, "He's got his own problems, his own insecurities. This job is his whole identity. He's overcompensating. He has feelings, too; he gets hurt, feels lonely. He and his wife just split up. He's nice to his dog." She imagined him at home, going to bed alone, wearing baggy pajamas and looking like a rejected loser. These thoughts and images helped change the way she perceived him.

C. Practice Being Diplomatic in Imagery

I asked Jessica to imagine herself at a meeting with him. She reminded herself that he had a lot of information that she could use. She focused on his positive aspects, making positive statements to herself about him. I asked her to ignore the things about him that she didn't like, and to find something about him she admired or thought was of value. She imagined herself dealing with him very diplomatically, complimenting him on some aspect of his work that had merit. In the conversation, she told him she was interested in a project he was doing, that she liked his approach, and wanted to talk to him about it. She said she had another project in mind and that she would like his opinion. He expressed interest in her career and gave her some helpful pointers.

D. Make Positive Statements

Then I asked her to make positive statements about being around him. She said, "Some players are better than others, but it takes eleven to make a team. He must be doing something right or he wouldn't have the position he has."

Soon Jessica felt more tolerant and comfortable with him. She was able to take advantage of her boss's knowledge and work with him in a productive way. Eventually she was given the interesting assignments she wanted.

WANTING TO BE A STAR: JUDY

Judy comes from a family in which everyone is an achiever. Her parents and brothers are doctors and lawyers. She has been an overachiever all her life. As she went through high school and college she was always head and shoulders above the class. If no one else knew the answer, she did. Judy had always wanted to be a successful businesswoman. She and her husband, a lawyer, married with the understanding they would not have a family. Theirs was to be a two-career marriage. Judy was trim and attractive, with a no-nonsense manner—very direct. She had a fast mind and no trouble getting a job as junior associate in the finance department of an investment banking firm. In the first three months all went well. She learned quickly, made good decisions and developed a lot of contacts. She had done a lot of research for one assignment and had come up with a piece of information she knew was very valuable. Instead of discussing it with her colleagues, however, Judy waited until a meeting that included all the company's top brass before divulging the information. She thought she'd get applause. Instead there was only dead silence. The senior associate and the vice-president exchanged glances and looked over at the other members in her department. They made no comment and moved on to the next topic. Judy realized she was out of line.

PROBLEM: Judy was used to being special. She was used to being "outstanding." She didn't share information, but used it to enhance her own image. In the corporate structure, where teamwork counts, this type of behavior worked against her.

Solution

A. Explore Belief System

Judy believed that being successful is the same as being outstanding. When you're better than other people, you don't need the help of other people; you can do it on your own. She needed to learn that in the corporate world the reality is that the more you contribute to your team, the greater are your chances of success. The mark of success is a winning performance by your team. She could still maintain visibility while she cooperates with her teammates.

B. Evaluate Self-talk

I asked Judy to make a list of the statements she was making to herself about her work situation. They were:

1. Keep what you know to yourself, then you'll get all the credit you deserve.
2. If I'm better than everybody else they'll notice me and I'll be on a fast track.
3. If I'm not outstanding, I'm nothing.

She examined these statements and saw that the first two are unrealistic in the business world and the third was clearly irrational. She rethought them and came up with more productive statements.

UNREALISTIC	REALISTIC
1. Keep what you know to yourself, then you'll get all the credit you deserve.	1. Sharing information is the whole point of a team, to generate new ideas. If I share my information with them, they'll be more likely to share theirs with me. Then we'll all get credit.
2. If I'm better than everybody else they'll notice me and I'll be on a fast track.	2. Yes, but to get on a fast track you must become an active member of a team. If I try to be a star, I'll be resented and excluded.

Judy challenged the irrational message with a rational one:

IRRATIONAL	RATIONAL
3. If I'm not outstanding, I'm nothing.	3. It's ridiculous to judge my worth as a human being by how outstanding I am. Besides, in this case, by standing out, I'm less. I get more power from being part of a strong team than from being alone.

C. Use a Model

Then Judy chose as a model someone highly successful whom she respected and was part of a team. She observed how he functioned. She saw this person was effective and successful without being arrogant or secretive. He was not "me"-oriented. He was confident of his abilities and self-assured. He shared his ideas freely with the group, and worked with his peers toward a mutual goal.

D. Praise Oneself

Whenever Judy made an effort to function as part of a team for a day, she praised herself: "That was a very successful day." When she succeeded in feeling like part of a group, and made contributions to the group, she said, "That was good. I worked well with the team and they like and respect me for it."

E. Monitor Oneself

If Judy was to change her behavior, it was important that she first make herself aware of her impulses to play the starring role. She kept a diary of daily activities at work, and noted particularly those occasions when there was an opportunity and the urge to score for herself. Then she practiced deliberately resisting those urges and rewarding herself when she did:

April 6. 10:30 A.M. Senior associate complimented me on the research report I submitted last week on Barco Industries. I played it real low-keyed, thanked him, and told him I would let the others in my department who worked with me know he was pleased with *our* work, which I later did, and rewarded myself with a long lunch hour with Sue and Carol.

April 8. 2:00 P.M. Received a phone call from Harold at Amalgamated Trust. He gave me a great lead, which I was tempted to work on solo. Instead I called in Bruce,

Shirley, and Carol to discuss a team approach. I didn't need to reinforce myself—their new positive attitude and warmth they showed me was reward enough!

When you are in business it's important to make alliances with the people under you because you never know when—next week or next year—you'll be needing them or when they'll be above you. If you are a manager you also need a group of effective and loyal subordinates. Start picking subordinates for your team as soon as you come to a job. You can take the successful ones along.

Later on, when Judy was successful, she established a network of people at her job. She was supportive of people working for her and built them up. They, in turn, formed a support group for her. She developed a strong department with them, and when she was promoted, she took a lot of them with her. One of them, who was promoted above her, became very helpful later in cutting red tape and supplying her with information.

Once, Judy came back to our women's group and reported how someone at work had tried to get an edge on her unfairly—trying to take over one of her projects. Instead of telling the boss, she went to her co-worker and had a talk with him. He really was way out of line, but she handled it with dignity and understanding. She was able to work it out with him. She knew that later on he'd appreciate it. She was looking at it in the context of building a support system and building herself a team, by finding people around her who would not want to harm her in the future.

GIVING UP: SANDRA

Sandra began as a receptionist at a large advertising agency. Although she was divorced and lived alone with her little boy, she was able to manage both work and a household quite efficiently. She is bright, ambitious, and has a good business head, and after only one year on the job they trained her as an account executive. For three years she was on one of their major accounts, an oil company. Trouble arose when a younger woman, Kate, came to the agency to work as her assistant. It soon became obvious to Sandra that Kate was after her job. She was using many tactics to try to make Sandra look bad. She also made efforts to get close to Sandra's boss. One afternoon when Sandra said she had to go home to look after her son, Kate said she would stay late and do her extra work. The new woman was obviously taking her place by making friends with her contacts on the oil account, and taking credit for Sandra's strategy recommendations. The problem got worse when the oil company began to bypass Sandra and direct their calls and correspondence to Kate.

Sandra began to view the situation as hopeless. She felt Kate was more aggressive, smarter, more charismatic than she. It seemed hopeless to stand up to her and solidify her position. She started to lose interest, withdraw, and get depressed. She began to let her work slide even more, feeling that she had had it.

PROBLEM: When the young competitive woman came in, Sandra lost her perspective, viewed the situation as hopeless, and gave up trying.

Solution

A. Evaluate Self-talk

Sandra made a list of the statements she was making to herself about the disturbing situation at work.

1. She'll do a better job.
2. Everyone will like her better.
3. She's more aggressive.
4. I've had it. I'm not what I used to be. I've lost my touch.
5. She has new ideas.

Then Sandra countered irrational statements 1, 2, and 4 with rational, positive ones:

IRRATIONAL	RATIONAL
1. She'll do a better job.	1. She may do some things differently, not necessarily better. We each have our own style. I can do as good a job as I've been doing and I can do better. I can always try a little harder. I've been a little complacent lately.
2. Everyone will like her better.	2. They've liked me in the past. There's no reason for them to stop liking me; I haven't changed. Perhaps I could give them a little more attention.
4. I've had it. I'm not what I used to be. I've lost my touch.	4. What is this thing, touch? If I want to work harder I can get results. The truth is I haven't been working hard enough. I've been taking things for granted.

She took a more productive view of the real issues:

REALISTIC	PRODUCTIVE
3. She's more aggressive.	3. It's true that she's younger and has more energy. That's no substitute for experience. I'm a seasoned pro. I can be aggressive when I want to be.
5. She has new ideas.	5. I've never had any prob-

lems getting new ideas. All I have to do is start generating them again. With my background that'll be no problem.

B. Use Thought-stopping

Sandra used thought-stopping because she found herself constantly brooding about the young woman at the office. She kept thinking: "She's going to take my job. I've had it. I'm finished. I'm not as good as she is." Soon she began to stay awake at night worrying. I recommended she experience the thought, then say to herself, "Stop!" and substitute realistic statements, such as "I know I do my job well. So long as I continue to be proficient, I've got nothing to be concerned about. I know just what it takes to be tops at this job." She also used some of the positive, realistic statements from self-talk.

C. Make a Plan of Action

Sandra had to do some more research to generate new ideas. She investigated some programs for environmental acceptance and for a new campaign strategy. Working closely with the research department, she came up with a new proposal for a campaign.

D. Learn Assertive Skills

To handle the situation with Kate, Sandra needed to practice using assertiveness techniques discussed in Chapter Five. We role played in the office and I coached her in dialogues such as:

KATE: Sandra. you run along home. I know you're worried about Bobby—and he needs his mommy. I'll finish up your work.

SANDRA: You're so thoughtful, Kate. But that's not necessary. You see, long ago I determined that my family life would never interfere with my career. Nothing short of an extreme emergency gets in the way of my servicing my accounts or my other job responsibilities. So you don't ever have to concern yourself about filling in for me. But thank you anyway.

SANDRA: Kate, I want you to know that I take a close, personal interest in all of my accounts. The oil account, in particular. You probably didn't realize that when you phoned Mr. Keller at their office yesterday.

KATE: Why, no, I didn't think it mattered.

SANDRA: It does. Very much. And now that you know, please don't contact their office again unless I ask you to.

KATE: I was only trying to be helpful.

SANDRA: I'm sure that you thought you were. But I need your help in other areas. In fact, I think we should sit down right now and clarify what those areas are. That way we'll avoid any future misunderstanding.

Sandra also made a special effort to cement good relations with her boss, and to keep a high profile for the good job she was doing.

In a short time she felt more confident at work, and no longer let the idea that someone else was after her job throw her. She felt much more in touch with her strengths. She also consolidated her position within the agency.

AFRAID TO COMPETE WITH MEN: SHARON

Sharon was in my businesswomen's group. During one of our discussions she mentioned that she had a slight problem at work. She was in the sales department of a large paper supplies company, the only woman in a group of five salespeople. She knew her products well and had studied the market. Because she understood buyer motivation and was a hard worker her sales were very high. She met her quotas faster than anyone else. But she noticed that the men on the team would get resentful when she did better than they did. They started to cut her in subtle ways, like not inviting her out for lunch with them or by making snide comments, such as "Here's Wonder Woman." Sharon began letting her totals drop because she didn't want them to dislike her. She recalled a somewhat similar experience in high school. She told us that she had always done very well in school. But when she was in junior high her grades began to slide because her social life was her priority and she didn't want to get branded as a "brain" or compete with the boys.

PROBLEM: Sharon was holding back from doing her best because being liked was more important to her than winning.

Solution

A. Explore Belief System

Sharon believed that men will reject women if women compete and win. She thought it normal for a man to take the lead and be the achiever.

B. Evaluate Self-talk

I asked her to make a list of the messages she was giving herself. She wrote down:

1. Either I'm a success in business or successful with men. But I can't be both.
2. They don't like me if I do better than they do.

3. They're all going to hate me. I'll be miserable if they resent me.
4. It's absolutely necessary that everyone in the world like me. It's important to me that all the men like me.

Then Sharon decided that statements 1 and 4 were irrational, and challenged them with positive, rational statements:

IRRATIONAL	RATIONAL
1. Either I'm a success in business or successful with men. But I can't be both.	1. I can be successful in business and successful with a man who is comfortable with a successful woman.
4. It's absolutely necessary that everyone in the world like me. It's important to me that all the men like me.	4. I can't be everything everyone wants me to be. I have to be who *I* want to be. Some men will resent me and some won't. This isn't a popularity contest. Everybody can't like me.

Sharon thought statements 2 and 3 were realistic, so she rethought them and came up with positive, productive messages:

REALISTIC	PRODUCTIVE
2. They don't like me if I do better than they do.	2. This isn't a popularity contest. They don't have to like me, but they can respect me, that's more important.
3. They're all going to hate me. I'll be miserable if	3. Some may, some may not. They'll get used to me, and

| they resent me. | I can live with their resent- |
| | ment. |

C. Use GPE for Being Rejected by Men

Because Sharon felt anxious I suggested she build a GPE hierarchy for being rejected by men and experience it in imagery. She saw herself in the following situations:

SUD	SITUATION
30	A male colleague doesn't say hello to her in the hall
40	In a three-way conversation two men talk across her
50	She walks into a restaurant and three male colleagues are sitting at a table; they don't invite her over
70	A group of men are standing in the hall talking, and when she comes up there's an awkward silence; then everyone walks away
80	A man is sarcastic to her: "Here's our local Wonder Woman."
90	All the men seem openly hostile to her

Soon she was able to imagine these situations without a great deal of anxiety.

D. Learn Assertive Skills

I suggested she also learn some assertive techniques so that she could handle herself appropriately without being intimidating. It was important for her not to be abrasive or defensive in her interactions with men. There was no need to let them know she was doing better than they were. Nothing would be gained by flaunting her success. She could say, "We all have our good days and our bad ones—our ups and downs." It was important that she continue to show them respect.

Sharon joined an assertiveness training workshop, which was very helpful. One assertive technique that worked well for her was "time out." The men only put her down because they saw it upset her. When she acted as if it didn't bother her, they stopped. On one occasion a male colleague remarked, "Oh, here comes our liberated woman." Sharon didn't miss a beat. She kept on with the business at hand. She gave him time out. She knew they were saying things to get a response. She said to herself: "They're trying to break my stride."

E. Humanize Men

It also helped Sharon to see her uncooperative male colleagues as sulking children. She imagined them as overgrown babies. If any of them started giving her a hard time she would imagine them in that way, and be amused rather than intimidated or resentful. "Poor man," she'd say to herself, "he still handles insecurity like an eight-year-old."

SPECIFIC PROBLEMS
15

THE REENTRY WOMAN

If you're returning to the work force after an absence, reentry may cause anxiety. You may be a middle-aged housewife whose children are grown or a young divorcée who needs to support herself. Perhaps you want to supplement your husband's income, now that your children are old enough to take care of themselves. Whatever your situation, there are many positive aspects to coming back into the business world. You will experience a tremendous potential for growth and a new, stronger identity. You'll have the opportunity to see yourself as a unique human being.

As a woman, you were taught to be a silent partner, someone who only helped others—maybe a precocious younger brother or husband. You had an investment in helping them to become somebody so that you would have some importance. It never occurred to you that you'd be somebody important on your own merit.

After your children are grown or other nurturing situations terminated, you may feel unwanted, undervalued, lost. That is the time to make a list of your assets. Don't omit any of the growth experiences you've had. Perhaps you like people and have worked well with people in the past. Maybe you're good at organization. Have you been managing a household? Organizing PTA meetings? Doing volunteer work? Bookkeeping for your husband? Taking courses? Many of the skills you take for granted are given fancy management names by corporations but require basically the same abilities.

Freshen Up the Skills and Assets You're Presenting

If you need them, get some solid, basic skills, such as typing or accounting. Take courses. Improve your skills until they're marketable.

Perhaps you're entering after a long absence. Don't pretend that you'll start as a manager. You may have to begin with a low-level entry job, such as clerk or secretary, and use that as a starting point. You've got to prove yourself, no one knows yet how good you are, you have to show it, so you should get a job where you can be visible. It's better to take a job where there's a chance for moving up in management, no matter how low paying. If you can't find a job that has opportunity for promotion, use a clerical job just to get experience, then move to another position that has more growth potential. Use the low-level job as a chance to learn as much as you can about the business and organization, and then decided what direction you want to follow.

Jill had left a disastrous marriage in the Midwest. She hoped to be a sales representative for a cosmetics company, but when she applied for the position she got nowhere. Finally she took a job as a salesperson in a large New York department store, which enabled her to learn the industry. After less than a year, she was promoted to assistant buyer. She used this position to make contacts and to get an education about the cosmetics business. She eventually saw an opening in a cosmetics company, took advantage of it, and with the experience she had gotten in the store, was hired as a sales rep.

Jill was only thirty. If you're reentering after a longer absence, remember that you have skills that a younger woman may not have. You may have interpersonal skills and ideas about organizing, which should give you more confidence. You've learned a lot about life that a younger woman hasn't, so wisdom is one of the assets you bring to your job. The real problem for the reentry woman is not that she's competing with younger women on the basis of age, but that they have fresher skills.

Now is the time for you to talk to career counselors and read about business. Chat with people in different fields and find out what's expected in different types of jobs. Several good books have been written about matching your skills and aptitudes to a position in the workplace:

What Color Is Your Parachute? by Richard N. Bolles (Ten Speed Press)

Back to Business: A Woman's Guide to Reentering the Job Market by Lucia Mouat (Simon & Schuster)

Toward Matching Personal and Job Characteristics (Occupational Outlook Service, Bureau of Labor Statistics, Washington, D.C. 20212). This free booklet discusses 25 abilities, from working with details to assisting the public, and matches them with 280 different jobs.

Assessing your skills and needs, by yourself or with the help of a career counselor, will help you make a sound decision about your goal. After you've decided what you want, go after it aggressively. You might want to consider preparing yourself with an M.B.A. A third of all graduating M.B.A's are now women. Competent women M.B.A.'s command a much higher salary than those without, and have a wider range of job choices.

If you're reentering the job market, fear of failure may be one of the obstacles you face now. You're putting yourself on the line to be evaluated objectively. It didn't matter if you made mistakes as a housewife, but now your work has visibility and can be judged by others. Fear of failure is an area of potential anxiety for many reentry women. You may have avoided occasions for failing for years. I suggest that you examine this area carefully in the behavior questionnaire. If you think it applies to you, you might want to explore the problem further and use the recommended techniques for dealing with it.

Also, remember that when you enter a large organization, you must subordinate yourself to the identity of the company if you want to succeed. You've been boss in your own home, but you're not running your own show anymore. You're valuable to the company insofar as you can be part of a bigger operation, and adapt yourself to other people's—your boss's, for example—style.

UPGRADING YOUR JOB

If you're currently working, it's a good idea to review your job situation every six months. Is your job helping you to develop? A hard look may show you that you aren't getting as much as you should from your present job, and it may be time to move on. The following quiz will help you make a decision.

	TRUE	FALSE
1. I envy other people's jobs.	_____	_____
2. I hate it when my lunch hour's over.	_____	_____

3. Things that used to turn me on about
   my job don't turn me on any more.   _____   _____

4. I make a lot of personal phone calls
   from work.   _____   _____

5. I notice many more faults about my boss
   than I used to.   _____   _____

6. Weekends and vacations seem like the
   only time I'm alive.   _____   _____

7. I keep asking myself lately, "Why bother?"

                                              _____   _____

8. I feel more tired at the end of the day
   than I used to.   _____   _____

9. I've stopped trying to improve the conditions
   of my job—such as a better desk, making more
   friends—I routinely go through
   my work now.   _____   _____

10. I don't take as much pride in my work
    as I used to.   _____   _____

11. A lot of tasks I don't bother finishing
    or barely finish.   _____   _____

12. I'm often late for work.   _____   _____

13. My attitude in the office seems to be
    carrying over into the rest of my life.   _____   _____

14. I seem to be doing my job mechanically.

                                              _____   _____

If you've answered true to five or more of these questions, you may have outgrown your present job.

First, ask yourself: What are my priorities? Personal or business? If most of your emotional and physical energy is devoted to your social life, you may not need a more demanding or satisfying job. It won't be realistic for you to look for a career job.

Next, ask yourself: How realistic am I? Am I willing to put the effort into training myself to get the kind of job I want? Do I want to bother? Do I have the energy? Am I that dedicated? It was obvious that Gina, who had scored nine out of fourteen on the quiz, was dissatisfied with her job as a secretary with a Wall Street brokerage house.

"I'd love to become a stockbroker and run a seat on the stock exchange," she told us.

"All right," I said. "Let's see what you'd need to do to prepare yourself. You'll have to become more knowledgeable in finance and basic economics. A few evening courses for a semester or two will give you a good background. Then you'll need to upgrade your image and start spending time making social contacts with people in the business who can help you."

Gina didn't seem too happy about the idea.

"School?" she asked. "That's something I'm not too thrilled about. Before I got this job, I couldn't wait to get *out* of school. I wouldn't do very well in a classroom. And as for new social contacts, my boyfriend complains now that I don't give him enough time. That could put a dent in our relationship."

I had to point out to Gina that until she was ready to make a commitment to put out more effort or to set a more realistic goal, she was better off staying with the job she had and reevaluating it in terms of her real priorities.

Now ask yourself: Is my timing right? You may be very short on money or the job market may be tight. The time of year may be wrong. Is the rest of your life stable enough for you to make a job transition now?

Fourth, are you getting everything you can out of your present job? Are there certain things about it you don't like and could change, but haven't? Does this job suit your particular talents? Have a conversation with yourself. Pretend you're describing your job to a friend, pointing out the benefits and the drawbacks of your job.

Fifth, do you have realistic beliefs? Do you think:

- If I hang in there, eventually I'll get promoted.
- This job is only temporary; I'm going back to school to train myself for something better some day.
- No use in trying to better myself. The only people who get ahead are the people with pull.
- What's the use, even if I do get the job, I'll flub it.
- If I do this perfectly, people will notice me and I'll get a promotion.
- I'm just not the executive type. No one is going to take me seriously as a boss.
- People like me don't have terrific jobs.

All of these unrealistic beliefs may be standing in the way of your getting a more satisfactory job. Are there personal reasons or problems you're trying to avoid by getting away from your present job: like some co-workers you resent because they've been taking advantage of you and you haven't been able to deal with them; or a supervisor you are terrified of standing up to, or a director who intimidates you so, you're afraid to risk being more creative or inventive?

Let me warn you, these may not be valid reasons for leaving one job for another. The sad truth is you may find yourself struggling with the same kinds of problems in the new job. Gratned, it would seem a lot easier to quit, but unless the situation is really more than you can tolerate, you'd gain more in terms of personal growth and self-esteem if you could learn to resolve the problems in your present job. These are just the types of problems the techniques I've explained in this book can help you with.

If you've decided that it's time to change your job, it's

important you get a fresh look at yourself. Start by introducing you to yourself and see what you discover about yourself. Review all of your varied experiences—work and nonwork related. All the things you've done and accomplished, no matter how unimportant *you* may think they are. Did you know that there are universities that award credits for life experience, because they recognize that knowledge is gained outside as well as inside the classroom? Evaluate your own life experiences in terms of learning experiences. Make a list of them, and see where your credits lie.

Next ask yourself where a person with those qualities would fit in the business world, and what jobs might be available within that field. One woman, who had little job experience, spent many years helping promote her artist-husband, arranging exhibitions for him, submitting articles on his work to local newspapers and trade magazines, setting up lectures at community centers and getting him invited to important social and cultural functions. Yet, because she'd never been paid a salary, she thought her experience didn't "mean" anything. After an objective viewing of her life experiences, she saw that public relations was a field she was ideally suited for.

In other cases you may need to build upon your basic skills or sharpen your talents. Talk to people. Investigate the possibilities of advancement in your own company. Then find out the job requirements. What are the skills you need for a particular job? Ask people who are working in the field, and see what skills they have. What do they know that you don't know, what skill do they have that you don't have? Subscribe to trade journals, join an organization. Start thinking in terms of the job.

Before you start interviewing, create an image of yourself in the new job. Try the job on for size. See yourself in the job five years from now. See yourself functioning in the job at a very different level. The pay is satisfactory. Do you feel comfortable with the people you associate with? Ask yourself: Is this job offering me a future, or is it a dead end? Is this the field I want to devote my energies to? If you can answer yes to all these questions, you're ready to train yourself, if necessary, and get the skills you need for the job you want.

Make a list of your plan of attack, your timetable, and pin it on the wall. Include the people you want to meet who will help you in the right direction.

The first thing you'll need is a good résumé.

THE RÉSUMÉ

Presenting your résumé is like presenting yourself in your Sunday best. You're showing off the best possible you, spotlighting those aspects of your abilities and experience that would be considered desirable assets in the field you're pursuing. When you've decided on the kind of job you want, prepare the résumé by choosing selectively from your background and skills so that they fit, as closely as possible, the qualifications you imagine the employer is looking for. It may be easier, but it's definitely not a good idea to use the same general résumé for several types of job. If you're going in for selling, emphasize one phase of your experience; if it's product development, emphasize another.

The heart of your résumé has to do with your job experience. If you're weak in job experience, then try to fill in with educational or volunteer experience, or anything that will reflect abilities, talents, or special qualifications relevant to the job area you're applying for.

The résumé should say to your prospective employer: This is what I can do for you.

Don't bother mentioning hobbies or personal information like your age, number of children, marital status, or health. The wording of the résumé should be action-oriented. Use positive, assertive words like *created, designed, managed, organized, produced.* You can use *I,* which makes it more personal, but keep your language clear and to the point. Don't use clichés.

Don't say why you left your last job or that you're currently not employed. Don't mention salary; you'll talk about that in the interview. Avoid negatives like "I dropped out of college."

If a formal résumé makes you look inexperienced, as it might, for instance, when you're reentering the work force, then you may be better off writing a descriptive letter summarizing all your related experiences.

A résumé should look neat and orderly, and show you at your best. It should be well-typed on white or cream paper. The important thing to keep in mind when you're writing a résumé is that a very busy person should be able to read it in a short time.

There are two types of résumé commonly used. The *functional* résumé states your experience by category. The *chronological* résumé, which is used more often, lists your experience in reverse time order.

A FUNCTIONAL RÉSUMÉ

Jane Doe
2345 Holly St.   Home: (312)555-2958
Chicago, Illinois 60611   Office: (312)555-9302
Objective: Desire executive position in public relations department of health-related public service organization.

Work Experience
Public Relations: Developed programs for American Red Cross, American Cancer Society. Organized seminars in public health education for American Cancer Society

	and American Lung Association. Directed press conferences and briefings. Also instituted new programs on teenage smoking, which were highly successful. Wide contact with television and print media.
Writing:	Prepared press releases, press kits for American Red Cross, American Lung Association. Wrote speeches for president and two directors of American Red Cross. Also prepared brochures, newsletters, conference manuals, employee handbooks, fact sheets.
Coordination:	Arranged 1978 American Red Cross Regional Chapter Conference. Coordinated advertising materials for Greater Illinois Council United Fund Drive, 1974.
Management:	Supervised staff of fifteen, Press Office, American Red Cross Illinois Chapter. Head of Telethon and direct-mail campaigns. Chief of press section, American Cancer Society, during largest press campaign in organization's history.
1974–present	Publicity director, American Red Cross, Illinois Regional Chapter
1973–1974	Assistant to the director, public relations, American Cancer Society
1972–	Researcher, publicity department, American Lung Association

Education
University of Pennsylvania Business School
Courses in public relations and marketing, 1968–1970
Bucknell, B.A. 1968
Majored in English, minored in sociology

A CHRONOLOGICAL RÉSUMÉ

Evelyn Smith
6161 Waverly Place   Home: (212)342-6895
New York, N.Y. 10012   Office: (212)593-7000
My ultimate goal is an executive position in the product management department of a national company. My immediate objective is to obtain a trainee position in which I will utilize my experience in product management, marketing research, and merchandising.

WORK EXPERIENCE

1977–present   Universal Food Corporation
Assistant to Product Manager. In my current position I supervise quality control of food products in packaged meats line. Implemented advertising and public relations efforts for that line. Initiated an innovative product refinement which helped increase sales in packaged meats line by 30% in 1979. I also acted as copy coordinator with supermarket executives, restaurant chefs, institutional cooks, to promote product line. Devised programs that used salesperson for company in national supermarket chain. Developed special promotional programs for East Coast retail stores. Directed staff of six.

1974–1977   American Food Products Company
Researcher, marketing department. I coordinated data for marketing strategy for food product line. Developed new methods of research that resulted in faster information processing. I provided recommendations for distribution and sales improvement plans.

1973–1974   New York Hardware Distributing Corporation
Administrative Assistant. I implemented direct sales to wholesalers and manufacturers. Developed experience with full product line, including building materials line of company subsidiary.

EDUCATION
1973: Boston University School of Business
Courses in financing, marketing and merchandising 1972: B.S. Brandeis University

When you write your résumé be specific and give a complete picture of your duties. Show how your career progressed, and what led to promotions. If a company you've worked for is not well known, you can explain a bit about it. Be aware also that the same job title can mean different things in different organizations. So you may need to clarify what your duties were.

List organizations you belong to, but don't give any that might prejudice an employer against you, or imply that you would cause ripples in the company.

Before you send your résumé out, have it checked by someone who knows the field you wish to enter.

The cover letters should indicate what job you want, and be addressed to the head of that department or to the company's personnel department. Use the letter to introduce yourself, to express the positive and assertive aspects of your personality. It should tie in what you've done and your background to the job requirements or the company's requirements. It should indicate your knowledge of the company's needs, problems, or interests. If you think you have something special that might interest them you can go into more detail about that.

PREPARING YOURSELF
FOR AN INTERVIEW

Your Voice

In Hollywood's golden era, when talkies began replacing silent films, a lot of actors and actresses found themselves out of work. What happened? Their voices began to be heard. All of a sudden, the hero, heroine, or villain were no longer believable when the voice that went with the image squeaked, lisped, or whined. That's just one example of how important the sound of a voice can be. How you speak is one of the first impressions a person has of you, and it may also be the last. How much confidence would you feel in an executive with a squeaky or breathy voice?

The best way to hear your voice is to tape it. Do this in different situations: when you're talking to your boyfriend on the telephone, a client in the office, and your boss. Then analyze your voice. Does it sound too soft? Too high? Breathy? Nasal? Do you mumble? Do you speak too loud or too fast? Is your voice flat and monotonous, without color?

IF YOUR VOICE IS TOO SOFT If your voice is too soft you're not using your chest resonators. Try this exercise: Place your open hand on your abdomen so that you can feel it vibrate. Then, as if you wanted someone across the room to hear you, repeat the following verse loudly, with an open throat, and feel the vowel sounds vibrate in your chest.

Fee, fie, foe, fum, I smell the blood of an Englishman.
Be he alive or be he dead, I'll grind his bones to
   make my bread.

Repeat this loudly, with as deep a voice as you can. Keep your hand on your abdomen to see that it rises and falls because you're breathing deeply. This exercise activates the chest resonators, which will make your voice richer and more mellow, and also give it the ability to project or carry. It helps you to sound more authoritative.

Make sure you are breathing into your diaphragm, and not taking shallow breaths in the upper chest. Stand up. Put your hands on your ribs. Breathe in to fill your diaphragm, then chest, so your ribs expand. Breathe in through your nose, and feel the air go into your diaphragm and expand the ribs. On a sibilant S, exhale. Repeat.

Pretend you're on a stage, and talk to the back of the audience.

IF YOUR VOICE IS TOO LOUD Find someone whose voice pleases you and emulate her. Use the tape recorder to practice modulating your voice. Loudness may come from pressing on your vocal cords. Try more chest resonance.

IF YOUR ENUNCIATION IS POOR Tongue twisters are very good for improving enunciation:
She sells sea shells by the sea shore.

The shells she sells are seashells.

Peter Piper picked a peck of pickled peppers.

IF YOUR VOICE IS MONOTONOUS Take some dramatic sections from Shakespeare and ham it up. Be the great Sarah Bernhardt. Give your voice permission to be more free. Then take one sentence and see how many different meanings you can give it. How you can make it funny, sad, satirical, sarcastic. Use the tape recorder.

IF YOU ARE SPEAKING TOO QUICKLY Try some relaxation. Many women talk too fast because they're afraid others will tune them out before they finish. Only speak when you have something to say. Realize what you're saying has validity and is worth listening to. Listen and respond to what the other person is saying.

Your Appearance

Your appearance is a statement you make about yourself to the world. The way you dress and make up says many things about you: I'm organized; I'm efficient; I'm dependable; I'm serious; I'm grounded; I'm businesslike. Or, by contrast, I'm disorganized; I'm casual; I'm haphazard; I'm superficial; I'm a pushover; I'm frivolous. Consider carefully the statements you want to make about yourself when you present yourself to the business world, and groom yourself accordingly.

Let's examine the image of a successful executive woman, whose appearance communicates the message: "I'm to be taken seriously." Try to see yourself in that image. Your hairdo is simple and neat, your makeup is low-key and natural; clothes are simple, elegant, and comfortable. You're in style, without looking like a page out of *Vogue*—in other words, smart without trying. If you're wearing a suit, it's well cut. Your shoes are smart but comfortable. If you can, carry your essentials in your jacket or dress pocket, and avoid a handbag altogether. If you are carrying a bag, you tend to appear awkward and inefficient.

Companies have unwritten laws of dress. Be sure you are familiar with those of your company, so that you're dressed appropriately. There are some general nos in office attire: avoid costume jewelry; large, flashy rings; stiletto heels; sleeveless blouses; low necklines; long fingernails; and, usually, pants.

Check your clothes for hanging threads, bad alterations, loose buttons, and so on. These indicate sloppiness, and might be a signal that you can't do your job properly. Never dress competitively with a woman boss, and never dress in imitation of a man. Look at yourself in the mirror as you would a stranger: Would you have confidence in that person? It's been said that if you want to make $40,000 a year, you should dress as if you're already making that much.

Remember that men's business clothes are as distinctly stratified as uniforms in the military, and men are aware of the degrees of rank that are implied in the hundreds of variations of their business suits. You might want to look at Betty L. Harragan's *Games Mother Never Taught You* and John T. Molloy's *The Woman's Dress for Success Book*. They explain the business "uniform" in detail. You must realize you're making a statement by the clothes you wear, and dress appropriately for your rank in your organization. If your company is traditional, choose your clothes accordingly. In an offbeat organization you can be more innovative.

Always look your best. It inspires respect. Dress up so people at high levels will feel comfortable with you, and you'll find your own confidence bolstered.

THE JOB INTERVIEW

You've gotten your research done, gotten your skills, made sure your look and style are right. Now you're qualified and it's time for your job interview. Before you go on the interview, we'll do what some trainers do with athletes: go through a rehearsal. To get the feel of the experience it helps to go on a few interviews for jobs you don't want, just for the practice. When you have an interview for a job that does interest you, find out from other people what this job entails. Look at the interview as shopping around: you want to know what the company's like, what their management style is, whether you'd fit in, what is required of you; and if your skills fit the job. A job interview serves two purposes: It determines whether you satisfy their needs and they yours. You must also feel that you will be able to work satisfactorily with your prospective boss. Often the interviewee is so worried about being judged that she doesn't evaluate whether she wants to work with the boss. You're there to take care of your needs, too. Find out if this job will advance your career. Can you learn things that will help your growth?

It's important that you go on your interview prepared. Read everything you can about the company. Sometimes an interviewer will ask general questions like, "Tell me about yourself " or "Why do you want to work here?" or "What do you plan five or ten years from now?" They're asking more to find out how you'd answer than to get factual information. When you respond, do it calmly and confidently, with good timing—without going into too much detail. Sometimes they may point out a specific weakness such as lack of skill or experience. Tell the interviewer how long it will take you to acquire that knowledge, then, mention a few of your strengths. At some point you may have a chance to ask about the company's future plans, or research or development of a particular product. This is where the research you've done on the company will be helpful.

When the issue of salary comes up, you'll probably be asked what salary you want. Ask them what salary would be appropriate for this kind of job. If you're given a range, ask for the high figure. But before the interview, you should research what others in the same position are getting. If you've done your homework you'll know what the going salary is, and you won't need to be afraid to ask for it. Salary negotiation is part of the interview, so don't be intimidated. Have a positive attitude about what you're worth. Realize that the amount you're asking is what you're entitled to. If you do your job then they're getting their money's worth. Remember that the interviewer's job is to get you at as low a price as possible. One way of paying you less than you're worth is to find fault with you. If the interviewer objects that you don't have enough experience or you don't have the credentials, let him or her know that you will get these skills, and stay firm on what you think you're worth. Don't be dissuaded.

Before you go on the interview, practice in imagery. Using the relaxation techniques, get yourself very relaxed, and then rehearse the scene in detail. See yourself dressed in a well-tailored fashion. You've done research on what the job entails, and have figured out where your experience would fit into the job requirements. You have a well-put-together résumé. So you are prepared, and that gives you confidence. See yourself sitting in the office, answering the interviewer's questions calmly, not talking too much, hands quiet, body in a relaxed, poised attitude, composed. You're making good eye contact, speaking in a steady, calm voice, thinking before you speak, measuring your words, responding appropriately, and sticking to the business at hand. You're feeling very calm.

Role rehearsal is also a valuable preparation for an interview. You can practice with a friend. Have the other person ask you for information, and respond the same way you did in the image.

ON THE JOB

Finding Out What Your Boss Expects

Now that you've got your new job, to avoid confusion and save your energy it's advisable to find out what your boss's priorities are and what he expects from you. Your previous boss may have run a casual office; your new boss may like an office where things are organized and logical, where scheduling and reports are neatly done, so it's important to know his or her style and adapt to it.

Stephanie was highly competent. She arrived on time and did every assignment as perfectly as she could. She attended to every detail that came to her desk, and even looked for more work. It was understandable that she was disappointed when another woman, who was her peer, got the promotion she had expected. What Stephanie didn't know was that her new boss wanted a socially competent person in the job, and social skills took priority over job performance. He wasn't sure that Stephanie could handle the social activities that went with the promotion. She had made the mistake of not finding out what her boss's priorities were. So get as much specific information as you can. Always try to be clear in your mind what's expected of you.

Time Organization

Organizing your time well is extremely important to your success. A few simple rules will help keep your priorities straight.

1. On Friday, if possible, make a list of what has to be done for the following week.
2. Decide which jobs someone else can do and assign them accordingly.
3. List in order of priority the jobs you must do.
4. Make up a weekly schedule with the approximate time necessary to complete each job.
5. For several weeks keep a schedule with the time actually required for each job noted. See what interferes with keeping to your schedule, and then analyze your plan to see if there are any mistakes or other factors that keep you from finishing.

Speaking in a Meeting

When you're going to speak in a business meeting, it's a good idea to rehearse your presentation. Try it out on a friend and get feedback. A few minutes before an important speech or meeting, allow yourself some privacy to collect your thoughts. You may want to do a brief relaxation exercise and take time to reduce tension, slow down, and feel calm. Breathe deeply from the diaphragm. Be sure you know what you're going to say and how you plan to say it. If it will help you to feel more secure, bring notes printed in large letters on index cards. You may not need them, but it's a good idea to have them.

While you're speaking, be aware of audience response. If they become restless or inattentive, change your pacing and tone of voice. Consider cutting down on the content of your talk or move to another topic. Lowering your voice occasionally forces your audience to pay closer attention. It's a good idea to sip a glass of water once in a while; it gives you a breathing spell, relaxes your throat, and clears your voice.

Training Your Secretary

The first voice people hear when they call an office is usually the secretary's. If you don't have an efficient secretary, no matter what you do or how well you do it, the caller will be left with a poor impression of you. Your secretary is an extension of you. She schedules your time, arranges your work, writes letters for you and does research. Often, however, an executive has to train a secretary to be competent. If you want an assistant who will handle a great deal of work for you, the following steps may help:

1. Outline the policies and aims of your organization to her and explain how your job fits in. Discuss the unwritten laws, points of view, and attitudes as well as problems of the company. Tell her where she can learn about its operation and your product or service. If she isn't curious about these things, she may be too nonassertive for you.

2. Your secretary should be familiar with your writing style so she can draft letters, reports, memos, and speeches. If you

want to delegate a great deal of responsibility to her, she can do research and a lot of routine reading in trade publications for you. She can organize what she thinks is pertinent into a file.

3. For telephone calls, let your secretary know to whom you're always available, from whom to take a message, and whom you'll call back.

4. Your secretary can make a rough draft of answers to your correspondence. It'll save you time, because then you need only edit her draft.

5. Take the burden of scheduling off your shoulders. Put your secretary in charge of it. Advise her when your meetings are arranged so that there will be enough time in between for other matters that may come up. You may find it helpful to keep two calendars, one for yourself and one for her. Before you come in each day she should have your schedule for the day typed and on your desk.

6. If you take a lot of trips, let her keep a separate notebook with all the information you need for each trip. Have her make herself very familiar with the places you may travel: the best hotels, the most convenient ways of getting there, the best restaurants. She should make all travel and hotel arrangements.

7. When you have meetings, let your secretary pull the material from the files beforehand, so you're well organized. Have her gather all the information you'll need—notes, correspondence, and so on—and keep it in a folder ready for you when you need it, and in enough time for you to prepare yourself for the meeting.

8. Tell her that if she has any suggestions about the scheduling or work approaches in your office, you'd like to hear about them.

Sentiment doesn't play a large part in business. If the secretary you've had as you climbed the corporate ladder can't do the current job efficiently, get her another job or let her go.

If you have a secretary who's competent but you and she simply don't get along, because of a power struggle or personality problem, don't let it continue. Let her go. If your secretary doesn't do her job well it will hurt your performance. But if you have someone really good, let her know that you hold her in high esteem so she'll take pride in her work.

Decision Making and Problem Solving

- You have two applicants for a job: one is older and more experienced, the other seems very bright and eager to get the job. You have to make up your mind which one to take.
- Your department is getting its work in late during certain times of the year. You have to decide whether to have the staff work overtime or request more temporary help.
- A new, smaller company has offered you a job at a higher level than the one you have. You don't know whether to take the new job or stay in your own company and work for a promotion.
- Your department has the highest turnover rate in the company. The boss calls you in and asks you what you're going to do about it.

How would you go about making these decisions and solving these problems? Is it difficult for you to make decisions? Do you find yourself becoming nervous or procrastinating? Or, if you make one, do you worry whether it was the right decision or do you ever backtrack and change your mind?

Part of being a good executive is being decisive, because people are looking to you for guidance and policymaking. But many woman have difficulty making decisions because other people—parents, husbands—have been making decisions for them. They haven't had the opportunity to develop decision-making skills. It's a simple way of thinking, and knowing how to solve problems will give you more confidence in your decisions. Sometimes the things that may be keeping you back from making decisions are fear of making mistakes or taking risks, always wanting to be right, fear of disapproval, or wanting everyone to like you. Here are some steps that will help you:

DEFINE THE PROBLEM First, slow down. Be calm. Get as much information as possible. See the problem from every angle. For whom is it a problem? When did it start? What seems to be the cause? See the problem through other people's eyes. You may have prejudices or habits that keep you from seeing it clearly. When you are information gathering, repeat back to people what they've told you, so you can be sure you've understood correctly. We all have our own frame of reference, and you may, at first, have heard something other than what was said.

Don't confuse the symptoms with the problem. For example, your department may be getting its work in late. Being behind schedule is the symptom, but the problem may actually be that you are understaffed, or that the office procedures are old-fashioned or that the software given to you isn't adequate. You must examine what's needed to get the work done on time. To do this, you'll have to break the situation down into all its parts, to analyze it, and look at all the variables. Make sure you've allowed yourself enough time to collect all the details.

CREATE ALTERNATIVE SOLUTIONS After you've gathered all your information, redefine the problem. Write it down. The way you solve a problem often depends on the way you define it.

Next, consider the possible solutions. Generate as many as you can. Unfortunately, we all have a set pattern we use for problem solving—often what worked in the past. We need to break this pattern to explore new approaches. This is "reframing" the problem, getting enough distance between you and it so you can see solutions you ordinarily wouldn't notice. You twist the problem around, turn it on its side, look at it upside down and inside out. When you approach a problem at work, look at all your options. Play around with possible results. Fantasize what might happen if you took one course of action as opposed to another. That way you will generate new ideas.

Ask yourself how somebody else would solve the problem. Put yourself in your boss's head or in the company president's head. What would their approaches be?

Try brainstorming. Think of every solution you can. Don't worry if it's impossible to carry out—just think of everything.

Use other people as sounding boards. Try out your ideas on them and see what they think.

Remember, exploring new solutions requires risk taking, which can lead to growth and creative thinking, so don't stay in the same old pattern. When you approach a problem, try to decide if it's a high-risk or low-risk situation. Think of it in percentages. Ask yourself, "What percentage risk is it? Ten percent? Fifty percent?" If there's not much to lose, it may be worth the risk. Possibly there's no risk involved but simply a different solution. Also, ask yourself if this solution is acceptable to everyone. It may be good, but if it antagonizes people it may be the wrong choice.

PUT YOUR DECISION INTO EFFECT First, ask yourself if this is the right time to implement the change; if not, when is? Sometimes the best choice is the decision not to do anything.

Once you've made your decision, submit the course of action you propose, in writing, to your boss or the persons involved. Use the following guidelines, or a similar format, for organizing your proposal:

1. Objective—Define the problem that needs to be solved.
2. Suggestion—Outline what you suggest as a solution, and how you propose it should be done.
3. Reason—Give all the reasons why your plan of action is the best choice.
4. Method—Describe, in sequential order, how your solution should be carried out.
5. Costs—Estimate what this will cost (it can only be approximate).
6. Time involved—State at what date the plan will be finished. (Remember to leave enough time for information gathering.)

Make your proposal as thorough and professional as you can. Also, once you've made your choice and begun to act, erase any other choices and pursue the choice that you've made. Follow through with the decision you've made, don't vacillate. It's a waste of your time and energy to look back and wish you'd done something else. You're allowed to say, "I sure made a wrong decision on that one!" In business it's better to appear a decisive person than an indecisive one.

Some Pointers from Successful Executives

A successful management career entails much more than just performing well at your job. The following tips come from some successful executives:

Learn the Unwritten Laws of Your Company
Every corporate structure has its own unwritten laws which don't appear in the policy manuals. These are the dos and

don'ts of interactions. Before you join a company, talk to
people who work there, and when you start working, observe
what the successful people do.

Know the Chain of Command, Formal and Informal

Watch for small hints: How's the furniture placed? Who
has the better furniture or wears better clothes? Who defers
to whom? Who does favors for whom? These signs will show
how the different executives relate to one another. The most
important thing for a successful executive in a new situation
to find out is the company's power structure: Who's on their
way up, who's on their way down, and who's not going anywhere? In short, who in the long run will be the ones to choose
for allies.

Once you've figured out the chain of command, be sure you
always obey it. Back your boss in his decisions, especially in
front of other people. If you need information get it from him,
not others. Don't go above him unless it's unavoidable. Never
embarrass him or show lack of respect, because others will
feel this is your style and they can expect the same from you.
Authority is something executives are very possessive about.

Find a Mentor

A lot of people get to the top by receiving a helping hand
and guidance from another—someone wiser, more knowledgeable, or better placed in the company. This is a usual
procedure in corporations, so find yourself a mentor. The person should be in a power position, someone who can show you
the dos and don'ts, help you with problems, and be on your
side in case you need it. By all means, choose a winner. But
look for them, don't wait for them to find you.

Work as Part of a Team

Lone Rangers don't do well in management. Businesses run
smoothly when everyone pulls together. A star player may be

picked for an exciting role to fill, but she frequently makes people uncomfortable. A person who rises in the ranks knows that she will go further if she does a good—not spectacular—job, gets along with everybody, and makes the team come first. A person doing the promoting may ask, "Can she do the job well?" But at the back of his mind is: "How well will she get along with the people in the new job if I promote her?"

Motivate Others

A good team member gets along with others and motivates them. There are many executives in top positions whose outstanding quality is that they can inspire others to do superior work for them. Their secret is that they know how to deal with people. They keep them happy and satisfied and know how to reward them right. They can make people feel wanted and valuable.

Be Diplomatic; Don't Create Ripples

A good executive is sensitive to the feelings of the people around her or him. Being a rebel with a cause may be okay for Joan of Arc, but she wouldn't have held up long in a corporate structure. Don't rock the boat. Winning a point isn't worth creating conflict over. Being right is not as important as keeping harmony between yourself and your co-workers. You have to keep in mind what you want to accomplish, and the best way to do it is not to alienate the people around you.

Build Yourself a Support System

Tennis, lunches, and theater dates with people you work with may look like socializing, but they are much more. A good executive uses her social life to build up a support system of people who can help her. First, decide who is important to cultivate, who can do you the most good, and plan how to meet these people and get close to them. Building networks allows you to trade information and favors. It's important to choose your friends from among your peers or those higher up the ladder, not from among your subordinates. Even though you had more fun in the old cafeteria, now you have to eat in the executive dining room. Rank is the name of the game in the corporate structure.

Become Visible

Be seen, be noticed. You can be doing a fabulous job, but if nobody knows about it, it won't do you any good. Make sure you're visible for the right reasons; you don't want to be noticed as a troublemaker, for instance. And crazy geniuses aren't appreciated in most industries except perhaps advertising or show business. You have to be your own public relations person from the time you come into the company. If you win awards or get promoted or do a good job, be sure people know about it.

Develop the Ability to Project Future Problems

You must constantly look around and ask yourself: What can go wrong? What's a potential source of trouble for me in the next six months? Five years? Where will the company run into trouble? If you anticipate future problems you can make plans accordingly. A good executive can intuit the potential problems, and how he or she would deal with each one should it arise.

Know When the Rules Can be Stretched

It is assumed, in business, that certain rules can be stretched in certain ways. You must know what those rules and ways are and exactly how far you can go, before you're actually doing something considered illegitimate. In football, a feint is considered fair. In business, you can mislead your competitors up to a certain point, and cleverly outfoxing someone, as in football, is often admired. However, there's a certain point past which cagey deception turns into dishonesty, or deviousness becomes fraud, and you, as a manager, must be aware at all times of what is permissible according to the rules of the game.

Have the Ability to Bluff

One executive I was interviewing interrupted his discussion to chew out an employee on the telephone. He lambasted the man, swore, called him an incompetent, and sounded as if he were about to pound his fist on the desk. Then he calmly hung up and resumed talking to me. Later I realized that he had no more been angry at his employee than he was at me. He had turned his anger off and on like a faucet.

This executive had developed the ability to bluff. He acted on a principle that might be formulated: When in doubt, holler. Others might find that not always telling the whole truth gives them an edge, particularly if they acquire a reputation for holding back facts. There are many other forms of testing people out. All methods of bluffing create a situation contrary to fact, such as false confidence on the part of your adversaries, false fear, or false beliefs that will lead them to act in a way that will benefit you. Bluffing throws others off balance, confuses them, or makes them doubt their information or their moves to date. Bluffing, like good poker playing, misleads your opponent. Of course, it is absolutely essential to know where bluffing stops and cheating begins, but for the most part bluffing is expected in business, and among men at least, a skillful bluff is appreciated and considered admirable.

A FINAL WORD

Remember, the socialization process that makes men and women different has given women different strengths. Women, in general, have better verbal skills than men. They are better listeners. They pick up nonverbal messages more accurately. They are more empathetic.

Today, corporation executives are becoming aware that these abilities are needed in management. The number of seminars and group programs aimed at teaching men these interpersonal skills is an indication of how important they are.

And let's not forget "woman's intuition" and her natural holistic way of thinking. Studies have shown that while men approach problem solving in a linear, left-hemisphere-oriented mode of thinking, women often include both left and right hemisphere modes in their conceptualization of solutions to problems. It's also true that gender gives women a strategic advantage. The presence of a woman in management or the executive suite can often throw a man off his stride. Realize this, and make the most of it.

You see how much you have going for you? Just think what you can be, then, once you've overcome the unproductive conditioned responses this book helps you deal with, and you are free to utilize your full potential of acquired skills and natural attributes. You'll be more than well equipped to handle the problems that arise as you work your way up to the top!

INDEX

preparation for, 279–82

Language, assertiveness and,
  135–38
Life experiences, evaluation
  of, 273
Long-range career planning,
  163
  failure in, 33
Losing
  being shattered by, 37
  GPE for, 156–57
Love, need for, 184–87
Low expectations, 34, 169–
  71

M.B.A.s, 268–69
Meetings
  preparation for, 287
  scheduling of, 287
  speaking in, 285–86
Mental imagery, *see* Imagery techniques
Mentors, 292
Modeling, 97–99
  authority figures and, 214,
    217
  nurturing and, 222
  for perfectionists, 241
  to raise expectations, 170
  rejection and, 186
  sexuality and, 176
  for teamwork, 256
Molloy, John T., 282
Money, attitudes toward,
  29–30
Mothering behavior, *see*
  Nurturing
Motivation of others, 293
Mouat, Lucy, 268
Ms. (magazine), 147

Negative self-statements,
  86–90
Nonverbal assertiveness,
  111–13
Nurturing, 39–40, 219–30
  behavior questionnaire on,
    50–51
  emotional satisfaction
    through, 222–26
  as problem behavior, 61–
    62
  by rescuer, 226–30
  unprofessional image
    caused by, 220–22

Office confrontations, 123–
  28
Operant conditioning, 70–71
Order giving
  assertiveness in, 128–32
  behavior questionnaire on,
    57
  passivity and, 172–73
  problem with, 65–66
  to uncooperative subordi-
    nates, 203
Organization
  behavior questionnaire on,
    51
  problem with, 62
  of time, 285

Passivity, 34–35, 159–73
  in asking for raise or pro-
    motion, 171–75
  behavior questionnaire on,
    51–52
  Cinderella syndrome and,
    160–64
  in identification with boss,
    165–69

302 • *Index*

in changing jobs, 140–44
contending with disap-
    pointment in, 153–58
dependency and, 145–48
fear of, 36–37
in leaving home, 149–53
problem with, 64
Role models, *see* Modeling
Rules, when to stretch, 294–
    95

Salary
    negotiation of, at job in-
        terview, 283–84
    research on, 133
Savvy (magazine), 147, 170
Scheduling, 287
Secretary, training your,
    286–88
Self-image, new, 213–14,
    217
    for nurturer, 222, 225
    for perfectionist, 245–46
Self-monitoring, 215–16
    of perfectionist, 239–40
    of teamwork, 256–57
Self-statements, 86–90
    on authority figures, 206–
        7, 210, 212–13, 216–
        17
    on competition, 258–60,
        262–64
    on criticism, 188–89, 191–
        92, 196–97
    on nurturing, 220–21,
        224, 227–29
    passivity and, 161–62,
        166–67
    of perfectionist, 233–34,
        236–37, 239, 243–44
    on rejection, 185–86, 191–

92, 199–201
risk taking and, 142–43,
    145–46, 149–51, 154–
    55
on teamwork, 251–52,
    254–56
Sexual put-downs, 41–42
Sexuality, 174–82
    behavior questionnaire on,
        50
    chauvinism and, 179–82
    problem with misuse of,
        61
    trading on, 41, 175–79
Shaping new behavior, 96–
    97
Silent Movie exercise, 112–
    13
Skills
    building new, 146–47,
        170, 173
    conversational, 135–38,
        151, 213
    list of, 133
    organization, 222
    for reentry, 267–69
    social, 226
    teamwork, 250
    for upgrading job, 273
Skinner, B. F., 70
Smith, Manuel, 110, 163
Social life, career position
    and, 43, 226
Specifying goals and actions,
    117
Success, fear of rejection
    for, 192–95, 198–202
SUD (subjective units of
    disturbance) 208,
    210–11
    on competition with men,
        264